WAYWARD SHEPHERDS

Wayward Shepherds

PREJUDICE AND THE PROTESTANT CLERGY

RODNEY STARK

BRUCE D. FOSTER

CHARLES Y. GLOCK

HAROLD E. QUINLEY

HARPER & ROW, PUBLISHERS

NEW YORK, EVANSTON
SAN FRANCISCO, LONDON

1817

Volume Six in a series based on
the University of California Five-Year Study of Anti-Semitism
in the United States
being conducted by the Survey Research Center,
Charles Y. Glock, Program Coordinator,
under a grant from the Anti-Defamation League of B'nai B'rith

Contents

Contents

Tables

FIGURES

Acknowledgments

This book is part of what has become known as the Five-Year Study of Anti-Semitism in the United States sponsored by the Anti-Defamation League of B'nai B'rith and conducted by the Survey Research Center of the University of California, Berkeley. By now this name is more than a little misleading, since the study has continued for nine years and the end is not yet in sight as new studies continue to be born out of the old. Our original inquiry into the religious roots of anti-Semitism was published in 1966. The questions raised in the discussion of the study eventually led us to reappraise our findings by undertaking the present work.

A number of persons made important contributions to this book. Sheila Babbie played a major role in designing the questionnaire and the sample. Jeffrey K. Hadden lent important critical advice on the last chapter, as did Scott Morris, of *Psychology Today*, in which excerpts of the chapter appeared. Camilo Femenias, Steve Johnson, Charles Yarbrough, and Alan Wilson each developed computer programs used for the analysis reported in this book. Heidi Nebel, Frank Many, and Margaret Baker all provided advice on data processing. For typing, our thanks are due to Katherine Lloyd, Eva Sinacore, and especially Beverly Fellows, who handled the production of the final manuscript in her usual extraordinarily capable way.

We are also indebted to Oscar Cohen, National Program Director

ix

of the Anti-Defamation League, who initially conceived of the whole research program, under whose auspices the authors have had a number of important dialogues with religious leaders about the meaning of our research findings, and who supplied a small grant to help pay for the present study. Finally, Heinz Eulau, of Stanford, provided counsel and funding for the study of clergy activism into which this study was grafted. Thanks to all of them, and to the clergy respondents to our inquiry without whose cooperation this book would not have been possible.

RODNEY STARK
BRUCE D. FOSTER
CHARLES Y. GLOCK
HAROLD E. QUINLEY

Berkeley, California
May 1970

WAYWARD SHEPHERDS

1

Christian Beliefs and Anti-Semitism— Revisited

In the spring of 1966 a study published under the title *Christian Beliefs and Anti-Semitism*[1]* reported that many Americans remain hostile toward Jews on religious grounds. The authors estimated that the anti-Semitism of perhaps as many as 17.5 million adult Americans was rooted in religious convictions that the Jews crucified Christ, remain outside of God's redeeming grace, and continue to be the objects of divine wrath and retribution. The study had two major thrusts. The first was an empirical demonstration that certain kinds of religious conviction with grave potential for producing hostility toward Jews were common among American Christians and that these religious conceptions were correlated with purely secular anti-Semitic beliefs and feelings (that Jews cheat in business and are subversive and unpatriotic, for example). The second major objective of the study was to present a theoretical account of the linkages between religious convictions and the development of anti-Semitic beliefs and feelings, and then to demonstrate that the theory was compatible with the empirical data.

The book received widespread attention in the national press and in religious and academic journals and discussion. Indeed, in a preliminary form, a report on the findings became an element in the evolution of the statement on the Jews produced by Vatican Council II. Along with attention, the study also generated controversy. Virtually none of the critics resisted the *descriptive* findings of the study. Religious and aca-

*Notes begin on page 123.

1

demic reviewers alike accepted the probable accuracy of the evidence that anti-Semitism persists in America and that Christian churchgoers are not immune to such prejudice. Similarly, there was ready acceptance of the distribution reported among Christians of beliefs that the Jews killed Christ and are ineligible for salvation. Objections were made to the authors' *causal* assertions. The idea that these religious convictions are a source of anti-Semitism became the main grounds for contention.

Perhaps understandably, reactions to these causal statements were highly correlated with a critic's religious outlook. Critics who did not hold religious convictions which corresponded with those identified as being connected with prejudice were prone to agree with the authors' position; indeed, many of them found the results a simple verification of the obvious, given the historical nexus between Christianity and anti-Semitism. However, critics committed to relatively traditional Christian views found the authors' assertions unconvincing, even repugnant. The results simply did not jibe with their personal experience: they saw no anti-Semitism in themselves. Moreover, many religious critics regarded Christian beliefs and anti-Semitism as inherently incompatible. There simply had to be something erroneous about a study which found otherwise, and consequently many such critics concluded that the authors had failed to study "authentic" Christianity.

Even among professional social science reviewers, private religious convictions seemed a major factor governing judgments of the book. Unlike their religious counterparts, academic critics did not make this issue explicit. Still, the book provoked as wide a range of reaction in academic publications as it did in religious ones and, it seemed, along roughly the same axis. For academic reviewers, too, the critical question was causality.

The popular image of science is that it constitutes a method for pursuing truth unambiguously and incontrovertibly and that this method is agreed upon and understood by all those who call themselves scientists. Like all popular images, it is partly accurate, fitting more closely perhaps the natural rather than the social sciences. But in all of science considerable disagreement persists on fundamental questions about the logic and methods of scientific inquiry. These disagreements become particularly prominent over questions concerning the proper basis for imputing causation, especially when the research cannot be based on controlled experiments. A great deal of social research obviously cannot be done experimentally.[2] But when studies attempt to approximate experimental controls by statistical manipulations, their authors must resolve many vexing problems of how to demonstrate causation and they must be prepared for considerable criticism from those whose preferred solutions to these problems differ from those used. Furthermore, the existence of such disputes within science serves as a temptation for those whose real grounds for objection are not scientific.

Among the reviewers of *Christian Beliefs and Anti-Semitism* there were some who shared the authors' views of the proper rules of scientific inquiry and consequently found the results persuasive. Others, with different methodological preferences, were not so persuaded. None rejected the possibility that the causal assertions made were accurate, but many critics felt the probability of this was quite low.

Arthur Stinchcombe has recently claimed that any social scientist worth his salt can think up at least five plausible explanations in five minutes for any particular empirical relationship.[3] Critics of the findings reported in *Christian Beliefs and Anti-Semitism* were clearly worth their salt. Their reviews abounded with plausible counterexplanations, that is, with reasons other than the ones the authors suggested for the relationships found. The real trick, of course, is not simply to think up explanations, but to discover which are false and which are fruitful.

In a general way the purpose of the whole scientific enterprise is to eliminate competing explanations by falsifying some of them. Indeed, in principle, we are never able to prove theories, but only to disprove them, and those we fail to disprove we provisionally accept as if they were true. Since critics offered many counterexplanations of the findings which directly contradicted the authors' own, an important step forward would be made if either ours or theirs could be falsified. In fact, one frequently cited counterexplanation of the data which proposed that authoritarian psychological tendencies caused both conservative religious convictions and anti-Semitism (and thereby concluded that the imputation of causation to religious beliefs was spurious) was empirically falsified by the senior author in a subsequent article.[4] Aside from this article, however, the authors did not debate their critics. For one thing, perhaps surprisingly, there is no convenient forum for doing so, and to request journals to publish letters of rebuttal is awkward, mainly ineffective, and somewhat demeaning. A more important reason, however, was that many criticisms could be tested only with additional evidence. The idea of collecting appropriate new evidence and attempting to replicate the original study did occur to the authors at the time. But by then Glock and Stark had become preoccupied with other lines of research, so they decided to wait for others to take up these questions.

This decision proved short-lived. When an unexpected opportunity arose to conduct a replication in a way which would permit settlement of many of the conflicts raised by the critics, the authors found they were eager to do so: it had the priority of old business.

A few words need to be said now about how this study came to be done and how it happened to have four authors. In the spring of 1968, Harold Quinley, then of Stanford University, consulted with Stark and Glock about a study of California Protestant clergymen he was preparing. His primary interest was in the sources and extent of clerical activism on behalf of social and political causes. In the course of our conversations it became clear that his study was well suited to provide a replication of the earlier research on religion and anti-Semitism, this time among the clergy instead of the laity. This was a most intriguing possibility. In a number of important ways, simply by shifting the investigation from the laity to the clergy it would be possible to assess many of the criticisms of the original study. In the initial study "the church" meant church members, and "religion" was what members believed and did. Now we could extend these definitions; "the church" would also include its professional representatives, and it would be possible to explore questions about the similarities as well as the exchanges between the clergy and the laity. (Such concerns will be taken up at length in subsequent chapters.) Quinley became interested in the possibility of building such a replication into his study—it would require only a few extra items beyond those he would need anyway—and agreed to collaborate. After a number of meetings on questionnaire design and selection of the sample, Quinley took sole charge of the data collection, which required the remainder of the spring and summer. Meanwhile Stark and Glock turned to other matters; their plans for analyzing the data and writing up the findings remained vague. In the fall Foster arrived at the Survey Research Center from England on a fellowship to complete his Ph.D. dissertation in the sociology of religion. One of his reasons for coming to Berkeley was to gain experience in quantitative analysis.

Late in 1968 Quinley brought over from Stanford a complete tape of his data. By this time Glock was away for a sabbatical year at Yale and Stark was involved in studying the police for the Violence Commission, so the data on anti-Semitism went unexamined for some months. After Christmas, however, Foster undertook some preliminary examinations of the data. The results were extremely interesting and when compared with results Quinley was obtaining at Stanford stimulated a desire to move ahead on the study. From then on the work was conducted in a series of short bursts of labor as all four of us squeezed it into our schedules. The result is this volume, based on 1,580 Protestant ministers randomly selected from the churches of California.

Since the main purpose of this book is to reinvestigate the arguments made in *Christian Beliefs and Anti-Semitism*, it is necessary to begin with a summary of the main theoretical arguments and empirical findings presented in that study. The next section of this chapter is devoted to that recapitulation. Those familiar with the earlier work may wish to skip over it. Finally, in this chapter we shall outline in more detail the design of the study and give a brief description of how the remainder of the book is organized.

Christian Beliefs and Anti-Semitism: A Summary

The basic proposition tested in the earlier study is a simple one, namely, that ideas have consequences. Certain interpretations of Christian faith, it was postulated, are conducive to producing specifically religious hostility toward Jews, and religious hostility, in turn, has the propensity to lead to secular anti-Semitism.

The beginning of this causal chain is orthodox Christian belief, a commitment to traditional and central doctrines in Christian theology. This theology postulates the existence of an active, personal, judging God, who imposes certain requirements on men. To believe in the divinity of Jesus Christ, through whom men may be redeemed and given everlasting life, is one of these requirements. Another, recognizing the universal applicability of Christianity, is that it be carried to all mankind.

This universality of Christian theology fosters a second link in the chain leading to anti-Semitism: a disposition to see Christian truth as the *only* religious truth. By implication, all other faiths are at least inferior and sometimes viewed as dangerous and wicked. Particularistic interpretations of Christianity, it was argued, produce a twofold response to religious outsiders. Initially particularism prompts missionary zeal; the faith is open to all mankind if only they will accept it. But when others reject the call to conversion, the hostility latent in particularism is activated.

This hostility is directed against all religious outsiders, whether they are of another faith or none. But because of their historic link with Christianity, the Jews are singled out for special attention and have lived for almost two thousand years as a visible and permanent religious minority in a sometimes militantly particularistic Christian culture.

This leads to the third link between Christian beliefs and anti-Semitism: specifically religious hostility toward Jews. This hostility, it was anticipated, would be manifested in a negative image of the historic Jews, not as unenlightened pagans, but as renegades from the true faith and cruel persecutors of the faithful—indeed, the very Crucifiers and revilers of the Son of God. It would also be evident in an image of the modern Jews as still bearing the stigma of and being punished for the alleged ancient "guilt" of their forefathers.

The final link in the causal chain is secular anti-Semitism. The orthodox Christian, led by his beliefs to a particularistic vision of Christian faith and thereby to a conception of the Jews as religiously illegitimate, would be especially vulnerable, it was expected, to secular anti-Semitic stereotypes and feelings. If one already believes a man to be a heretic or an enemy of God, one is hardly surprised that he is also untrustworthy, subversive, and an egomaniac.

These theoretical ideas were subjected to tests in the earlier study through two data collection operations: (1) an extensive survey of a probability sample of three thousand Christian church members in the San Francisco Bay Area in which respondents answered a lengthy questionnaire requiring on the average three hours to complete; (2) a survey consisting of two thousand personal interviews of a representative sample of the adult population of the nation. This second survey was undertaken in order to exclude any possibility that the original findings had been the product of regional oddities of Northern California or sample bias or the result of random error.

The results of both surveys provided confirmation of the theoretical model. There is considerable variation among Christian churchgoers and in the population at large in the extent of commitment to traditional Christian dogma. Orthodoxy, defined as unwavering belief in the existence of God, the divinity of Jesus, the existence of an afterlife, and the Biblical miracles, remains the dominant form of commitment. However, doubt and disbelief also characterized many subjects.

Both samples also showed variation in the extent to which persons are particularistic about their faith. At one extreme were those who conceive that belief in Jesus Christ is absolutely necessary for salvation, that salvation can be achieved only by being a member of the Christian faith, and that being completely ignorant of Christ, as might be the case for people living in other countries, would prevent salvation. At the other extreme were those who reject the idea of salvation altogether and hence have no particularistic vision of Christianity.

On the average, subjects were about as likely to be highly particularistic as to exhibit little particularism, but this varied considerably according to how orthodox they were. Confirming the authors' hypothesis, orthodox believers were much more highly disposed to be particularistic than nonorthodox ones. Sixty per cent of Protestant churchgoers who scored high on orthodoxy also did so on particularism, while only 6 per cent of the least orthodox did so. Conversely, 58 per cent of the least orthodox scored low on particularism, as compared with 4 per cent of the most orthodox. A similar pattern was observed among Roman Catholics.

Turning to the third link in the postulated chain—religious hostility toward Jews—it was found that the traditional image of the historic Jew as Crucifier remains widespread; a majority of both Catholics and Protestants in the church-member sample and almost as many in the national sample continue to single out the Jews as the group most responsible for crucifying Christ. At the same time, the Jewish legacy of the Old Testament is somewhat forgotten; indeed, a small minority Christianize the entire Biblical tradition.

Some people, the authors discovered, are able to assign negative and wicked motives to ancient Jews without harboring ill will toward modern Jews or regarding them as heirs to their ancient "guilt." For them, what they believe the Jews did two thousand years ago is ancient history, as unrelated to modern feelings between Christians and Jews as the Revolutionary War is between contemporary Americans and the British. But not all Christians feel this way. A substantial minority consider the modern Jew as still suffering under a divine curse called down upon themselves, as reported in the Book of Matthew, at the Crucifixion.

Making this link between the ancient and modern Jews is especially characteristic, it was found, of orthodox believers who hold a particularistic conception of Christian religious supremacy. For example, 77 per cent of Protestant churchgoers of this persuasion agreed that "the Jews can never be forgiven for what they did to Christ until they accept him as the True Saviour," whereas only 1 per cent of the nonorthodox and nonparticularist thought so. Among Roman Catholics, the findings were also consistent with the theoretical expectations, but the effects were not so dramatic. Thirty-three per cent of the highly orthodox and particularist Catholics agreed with the foregoing statement; none of their opposite number did.

To this point, all tests of the theory were confirming. Orthodox faith that claims universal truth and specifies in detail what that truth is leads persons to take a particularistic conception of their religious status. Particularism leads Christians to be especially negative in their historic image of the ancient Jew, to see the Jews as wickedly implicated in the Crucifixion of Christ. The combination of these factors predisposes Christians to hold a negative religious image of the modern Jew as unforgiven for the "sins" of his ancient forebears and as suffering God's eternal punishment.

The final link in the causal chain to be tested was anti-Semitism per se. However conceived and measured, whether as negative beliefs about Jews, ill feelings toward them, or a predisposition to act in a hostile manner toward them, anti-Semitism is far from extinct among churchgoers or in the population at large. In the California church-member sample, the authors judged a third of the Protestants and almost as many Catholics (29 per cent) to be moderately or highly anti-Semitic at an attitudinal level. The measures used in analyzing the data from the national sample were not strictly comparable, but a third of the sample expressed agreement with a majority of outrightly negative anti-Semitic stereotypes.

The vital question, of course, was whether those caught up in the causal chain would be more likely to be anti-Semitic than those who were not. In both samples, it was found that they were. Seventy-eight per cent of the California Protestant churchgoers, and 83 per cent of

the Roman Catholics who were orthodox and particularistic in their faith
and had expressed religious hostility toward Jews, revealed themselves
to be moderately or highly anti-Semitic. Among their nonorthodox, non-
particularistic, nonreligiously hostile counterparts, only 10 and 6 per
cent, respectively, scored as moderately or highly anti-Semitic. The
results in the national sample for both Protestants and Catholics were
roughly equivalent.

Crucial to these relationships was religious hostility toward Jews.
While orthodox and particularistic Christians were extremely likely to
hold a hostile religious image of the modern Jew, and if they so did, to
embrace anti-Semitic beliefs generally, if their particularism did not link
the modern Jew with the "sins" of ancient Jewry, they were very unlikely
to exhibit anti-Semitism. Thus, religious hostility was found to be the piv-
otal factor in the process leading from Christian beliefs to anti-Semitism.

Having shown that the correlations predicted among the various parts
of the process leading from religious beliefs to anti-Semitism were empirically supported, the researchers still faced the question whether they
occurred for the reason suggested or on other grounds. Was religion a
cause of anti-Semitism, or were the two linked because some other
antecedent factor was leading people both to this combination of Christian beliefs and independently to anti-Semitism?

Perhaps the strongest confirmation of the theory that religion plays
a role in generating anti-Semitism was provided by examining the relationship between the religious variables in the causal chain and attitudes
toward Negroes. Many studies have established that prejudiced attitudes
toward Jews and Negroes, as well as against other religious and ethnic
groups, are very highly correlated. This study, however, was not attempting to account for anti-Semitism in general, but to uncover and isolate
specifically religious sources for prejudice against Jews. Since Negroes
are largely Christian, these same religious factors ought *not* to operate
to generate hostility toward them. In effect, to the degree that purely
religious sources of prejudice had been successfully uncovered, the model
ought to fail to account for racial prejudice.

The data showed this to be the case: the religious variables in the
causal chain did not predict attitudes and beliefs toward Negroes,
despite the fact that anti-Semitism and anti-Negro prejudice are highly
related. Thus, the authors argued, the study successfully isolated some

purely religious sources of anti-Semitism and had not merely tapped some general ethnocentric syndrome.

Further tests of the theory eliminated such measures of social class as education, income, and occupation as possible alternative explanations. While a person with a Ph.D. degree was unlikely to hold highly orthodox and particularistic religious views, if he did he was as likely to be anti-Semitic as were persons who had failed to complete the eighth grade and also hold such religious views.

Similarly, controls for age, sex, political affiliation, and rural and urban origins failed to alter the basic relationship between religious ideas and anti-Semitism.

It appears, then, that religion not only played a crucial role in the rise of anti-Semitism but even today continues to reinforce and foster hatred of the Jews—so much so, the authors judged, that at least one-fourth of America's anti-Semites have a religious basis for their prejudice, while nearly another fifth of them have this religious basis in considerable part. Indeed, only 5 per cent of Americans with anti-Semitic views lack all rudiments of a religious basis for their prejudice. On these grounds, it seemed reasonable to say that if the explanation of the empirical findings was correct, an impressive proportion—no less than a fourth—of American anti-Semitism is generated from religious sources; this means, as was stated at the beginning of the chapter, 17.5 million adult Americans.

In conclusion, the earlier study confronted the question of what might be done constructively to break down or to derail the process by which religious belief fosters anti-Semitism. It was recognized that one possible point of attack would be to shatter the syndrome at its source through a theological rejection of Christian orthodoxy and particularism. A solution of this kind, however, seemed unacceptable and unrealistic. Those strongly committed would not yield their beliefs easily, nor would it be legitimate to ask them to do so.

However, the authors did think it possible to reduce the tendency for orthodox believers to become particularistic. Orthodox Christians are highly prone to be particularistic, but this is not true for everybody. How orthodox persons restrain themselves from taking up a particularistic view of their own religious superiority was not wholly explained by the data. It was discovered, however, that for many the answer seems to be their commitment to ideals of religious liberty. Effectively taught, religious liberty might be made an ever more effective instrument to forestall orthodox theology from becoming particularistic.

The causal link between faith and anti-Semitism cannot be wholly severed as long as particularism remains a dominant theme in Christianity. It might be significantly muted, however, if the deicide issue could be laid to rest once and for all. An invidious interpretation of the role of the Jews in the Crucifixion is an important link between particularism and religious hostility toward the modern Jew. Without the reinforcement provided by the deicide tradition, less hostility might be generated by particularism, though the simple fact that Jews remain outside the true faith would be enough to sustain a degree of hostility.

The final point at which the process by which faith is translated into anti-Semitism ought to be attacked, the authors felt, is in the stereotypes and feelings making up anti-Semitism itself. While the data showed that the church often provides the ground in which anti-Semitism grows, nothing suggested that the church is directly promoting secular anti-Semitism. Finally, then, it was proposed that a massive frontal attack carried out by the churches on anti-Semitism per se could have leverage in reducing all hatred toward Jews, whether based on religious grounds or not.

Figure 1 summarizes the explanatory model; the arrows indicate the postulated causal sequence. As will be clear in subsequent chapters, the model is intentionally simplified to facilitate an overview of the main argument. To summarize briefly, the process begins with Christian orthodoxy. Inherent in orthodoxy is an exclusive conception of religious legitimacy, which we have called particularism. To orthodoxy and particularism are added the historic and Gospel images of the Jews as those who rejected Christ and, indeed, engineered his Crucifixion. For orthodox and particularistic Christians these hostile images of the historic Jew retain their relevance for evaluations of the contemporary Jew. Thus many Christians define the Jews as still suffering from the guilt of the Crucifixion and as the objects of divine wrath and retribution. Finally, this hostile religious image of the modern Jew invites commitment to secular anti-Semitic stereotypes: Jews as immoral, dishonest, disloyal— the whole lexicon of bigotry.

Details of the Replication

The question of the actual role of the churches in promoting religious hostility toward Jews or in combating anti-Semitism can now be assessed.

The theoretical model developed in the earlier study will be confronted with empirical data based on the clergy to see how well it applies. We do not anticipate that the clergy will be descriptively identical with the laymen on all major components of the model. Because of their greater average education, the clergy as a whole should be less anti-Semitic than the laity. And we expect that the clergy, because of their greater theological sophistication, will be less prone to invidious interpretations of the Crucifixion story. But despite some such variations we still expect to find the elements of the model correlated among the clergy in the same

Figure 1. CAUSAL SEQUENCE:
ORTHODOXY TO ANTI-SEMITISM

way as among laymen. If this is not the case, a number of the earlier explanatory assertions will be falsified. That, of course, is precisely the purpose of the replication: to submit the authors' explanation and important counterexplanations offered by the critics to an empirical survival test.

In designing the replication we included essentially the same questions previously used in the studies of laymen. We did not ask as many questions because the earlier analysis had isolated the important ones. The universe from which the sample was drawn included all parish clergymen of the nine largest Protestant denominations in California. All ministers serving in California in these denominations were in the original sampling frame, and approximately 80 per cent of them were randomly selected to receive the mail questionnaire in the spring of 1968. Appropriate follow-up mailings were sent to encourage nonrespondents to answer. An over-all response rate of 63 per cent was finally achieved, and 1,580 clergymen returned completed and usable questionnaires. A special assessment was made of a randomly chosen subsample of nonrespondents in an effort to determine what, if any, bias may have operated in the returns. This showed there was a modest tendency toward overrepresentation of younger and more theologically liberal clergymen.[5] Any researcher would prefer a 100 per cent return rate (thus no possibility of sample bias) or at least no detectable biases in the returns received. This is not often possible with mail questionnaires. Nevertheless, the biases detected do not prohibit analysis *because they work against the hypotheses we shall attempt to demonstrate*. Because of biases in the returns, we shall report *underestimates* of the prevalence of traditional religious beliefs, hostile religious images of Jews, and prejudice among the clergy. This raises the possibility of hypotheses being falsified when in fact they would have been confirmed by a full sample. But it makes it implausible that the reverse could occur. If there must be biases, this is how they ought to operate. It is customary in science to maximize the difficulty of confirming one's own hypotheses. The biases in the data increase, rather than decrease, the rigor of the test.

Organization of the Book

Like the original study, the book is organized around the theoretical chain of factors which, it was postulated, links Christian doctrines with anti-Semitism. Chapter 2 examines the first two links in the chain: orthodoxy and particularism. Chapter 3 is devoted to religious conceptions of the Jews. In Chapter 4 the religious components are assessed to see what connection they have with secular anti-Semitism. Finally, Chapter 5 reassesses the role of the clergy and the churches as a source of moral guidance. At appropriate points along the way objections raised by critics to explanations of the lay data will be introduced and tested. The results as well as other points at issue will be summarized at the end of Chapter 4.

2

Theological Convictions

This chapter will assemble, describe, and explore relations between the first two factors in the chain which we postulate as leading from Christian commitment to secular anti-Semitism. The first link is orthodoxy, by which we mean acceptance of the central tenets of the historic gospel message: God the Father; Jesus Christ "His Son"; the promise of eternal life; and the existence of the demonic. The second is particularism, the traditional Christian position that it is the one and only true faith—that redemption comes only through Christ. We shall analyze the extent to which contemporary Protestant clergy accept orthodox views, then examine the validity of the Orthodoxy Index as a measure of the theological outlook of clergymen. Subsequently, we shall investigate clerical commitment to particularism and the extent to which particularism is a consequence of orthodoxy. Throughout, the clergy will be compared with the earlier findings for laymen[1] and reassessment will be made of previous judgments on the nature and extent of denominationalism in present-day America and on the degree to which secularization has taken place.

Clerical Orthodoxy

The obvious starting point in any assessment of what contemporary Protestant clergy believe is their beliefs about God. Certainly, the concept of a universal, all-knowing, and judging personal God is the bedrock of

15

the Christian-Judaic tradition. But, in light of the present ferment in modern theology, it can no longer be taken for granted that Christian clergy universally hold such a conception of God. Indeed, reconceptualizations from a "God up there," in Bishop Robinson's words, to a Tillichian conception of God as the "ground of being," or similar non-personal conceptions, are not restricted to the clergy.[2] Sharp divisions were found among the laity over their conception of God and the certainty with which they held their belief in Him.

Table 1 shows that two-thirds of the Protestant clergy in our sample reported unwavering faith in a traditional conception of God (as compared with 71 per cent of Protestant laity in the California sample). Several conclusions can be drawn from these data. First of all, as one might expect, modernist reconceptualizations of God are probably most common among theologians, at most only a third of the general clergy have to some degree responded to this movement. Whether or not this is a significant proportion depends largely on one's value commitments. Still, it is obvious that doubts concerning God and disbelief in Him are concentrated in a few denominations. Fewer than half (45 per cent) of the United Church of Christ clergy claimed they had no doubts about the existence of God, as did slightly more than half (52 per cent) of the Methodists. The Episcopalians, Presbyterians, and both American Lutheran bodies are close to the over-all average, while unwavering faith reaches 82 per cent among American Baptist clergy, 89 per cent of the Missouri Synod Lutherans, and an overwhelming 97 per cent of the Southern Baptists. Thus, on the most central tenet of Christian doctrine very large differences exist among the clergy of Protestant denominations. These findings are remarkably similar to the earlier results for the laity, as can be seen at the bottom of Table 1, where we have reported the proportion of laity acknowledging a firm belief in God's existence.[3]

The majority of clergymen who did not report unwavering faith in God did not choose to accept a different image of God, but simply admitted having some doubts about the existence of a personal God. One-fifth, over all, chose this answer (No. 2 in Table 1). Indeed, only 2 per cent of all the clergy said they did not believe in a personal god, but in some kind of "higher power"—6 per cent of United Church of Christ ministers and 4 per cent of the Methodists chose this response. Furthermore, the last line in the table provides a hint that this small

Table 1. MINISTERS' BELIEF IN GOD

Reply to: "Which of the following statements comes closest to expressing what you believe about God?"[a]

Response Category	United Church of Christ	Methodist	Episcopal	Presbyterian	Luth. Church in Amer.	Amer. Luth. Church	American Baptist	Missouri Lutheran	South. Baptist	Total
1. "I know God really exists and I have no doubts about it."	45%	52%	64%	63%	67%	67%	82%	89%	97%	67%
2. "While I have doubts, I feel that I do believe in God."	35	29	21	24	17	19	12	7	2	20
3. "I find myself believing in God some of the time, but not at other times."	2	1	2	2	1	2	1	0	0	1
4. "I don't believe in a personal God, but I do believe in a higher power of some kind."	6	4	1	2	1	0	0	0	0	2
7. "None of the above."	12	12	11	8	14	11	4	3	1	9
No answer	0	2	1	1	0	1	1	1	0	1
Per cent	100	100	100	100	100	100	100	100	100	100
Number	(137)	(354)	(207)	(226)	(87)	(118)	(147)	(134)	(170)	(1,580)
"I know God really exists and I have no doubts about it" (Response of Northern California lay sample). Per cent	42[b]	60	64	75	73[c]		79	81	99	71
Number	(151)	(415)	(416)	(495)	(208)		(141)	(116)	(79)	(2,021)

[a] Response categories 5 and 6, "I don't know whether there is a God and I don't believe there is any way to find out" and "I don't believe in God," received no endorsement.
[b] Percentage based only on those church members who answered the question.
[c] On lay analyses, results for Lutheran Church in America and American Lutheran Church were combined.

percentage of ministers in "liberal" denominations who openly reject a personal God is somewhat misleading. The proportions who refused one of the response categories provided in the item and devised an answer of their own (No. 7 in the table) falls sharply from left to right across the table. The following option was provided: "None of the above represents what I believe. What I believe about God is_____."
Now, while 9 per cent of all ministers chose to write in their own belief statements about God, only 1 per cent of the Southern Baptists and 3 per cent of the Missouri Synod Lutherans, as contrasted with 14 and 11 per cent among the two American Lutheran groups and 12 per cent among Methodists and the United Church of Christ, did so. Analysis of these individual responses showed that virtually all (at least 90 per cent) were of the modernist, "nonpersonal God" variety. A great many mentioned Tillich's "ground of our being" definition. Some said things akin to "God is in the human need and capacity to transcend oneself in love and compassion." If these responses are added to those of the fourth category, nonsupernatural conceptions of God are held by an appreciable minority of clergy in the denominations on the left side of the table: 18 per cent of the United Church of Christ clergy, 16 per cent of the Methodists, 12 per cent of the Episcopalians, and so on.

If faith in God varies among Protestant clergy, belief in the divinity of Jesus differentiates them even more. As is shown in Table 2, only 31 per cent of the United Church of Christ clergy and 36 per cent of the Methodists reported unwavering faith in Jesus, while 90 per cent of the Missouri Synod Lutherans and 96 per cent of the Southern Baptists had no doubts that "Jesus is the Divine Son of God." Over all, 61 per cent of the clergy had no doubts about Christ. This closely corresponds to the California Protestant laymen (69 per cent), and, again, the denominational patterns are virtually identical with those of the laity: for example, 40 per cent of United Church of Christ laymen and 99 per cent of Southern Baptist laymen gave this same response.

Further, as with the item on God, the largest group of those who failed to indicate unwavering faith accepted the traditional image of Jesus as divine, but admitted having some doubts (18 per cent over all). And again, use of the last category to write in an original answer was heavily concentrated among clergymen in "liberal" denominations. As in the question on God, these answers were overwhelmingly modernist.

rized thus: "I believe that the historic
ot the divine character of his message
edemptive suffering." Added to cate-
responses would indicate that a very
najor liberal denominations (40 per
ergy, 39 per cent of the Methodists,
dians) hold what is an essentially
object of symbolic veneration, but of

s our insight into the extent to which
ologized by the clergy of many Protestant clergy believed literally in the
ontrasts approach statistically possible
ch of Christ clergy, 14 per cent of
opalians, 80 per cent of American
therans, and 98 per cent of Southern
rally true." While in denominations
ace of the Virgin Birth is virtually
f Jesus (as well as the existence of a
able acceptance of the Virgin Birth
claimed unwavering belief in Christ.
several of these major denominations

ho literally believe that Jesus walked
pattern. While virtually all clergymen
viewed this miracle as literally true,
ations on the left side accept this
's divinity.
elief in Christ in terms of either the
ology or general acceptance of Jesus
ns such as Missouri Lutherans and
hern) are characterized identically.
he United Church of Christ, Meth-
ran Church in America, the picture
ask the general question or examine

l per cent of the United Church of

The modal answer could be summ
Jesus was simply a man, but I acc
and the symbolic meaning of his
gories 3 and 4 of this item, such
sizable minority of the clergy in
cent of United Church of Christ
and 21 per cent of the Episco
demythologized view of Jesus: an
man, not literally of God.

Indeed, Table 3 greatly increas
views of Christ have been demyth
estant bodies. Only half of all Pro
Virgin Birth. Interdenominational c
limits: 8 per cent of United Chu
Methodists, 38 per cent of Epis
Baptists, 96 per cent of Missouri L
Baptist ministers responded, "Lit
on the right of the table accepta
identical with belief in the divinity
personal God), on the left of the
falls far below the proportions who
Indeed, almost none of the clergy in
accepted the Virgin Birth.

The proportions of the clergy v
on water follow an almost identical
on the right-hand side of the table
almost none of those in denomir
traditional Christian proof of Chris

Whether we judge traditional b
major elements in the historic Chris
as Christ, conservative denominati
Baptists (both American and Sou
But among such denominations as
odists, Presbyterians, and the Luth
is variable, depending on whether w
specific elements of the Christolog

Thus we would estimate that 3

Table 3. ADDITIONAL BELIEFS ABOUT JESUS

	United Church of Christ	Metho-dist	Epis-copal	Presby-terian	Luth. Church in Amer.	Amer. Luth. Church	American Baptist	Mis-souri Lutheran	South. Baptist	Total
"Jesus was born of a virgin." Per cent who responded "Literally true"	8	14	38	42	52	75	80	96	98	50
"Jesus walked on water." Per cent who responded "Literally true"	8	14	36	39	51	76	77	94	97	48

Christ clergy, 36 per cent of the Methodists, and 62 per cent of the Episcopalians retain unwavering faith in the divinity of Jesus if we relied on the general item (shown in Table 2). But our estimates would shrink considerably to 8, 14, and 38 per cent, respectively, if we gauged commitment to belief in Christ on the basis of acceptance of His Virgin Birth. Similar reductions occur if we judge on the basis of belief that Jesus walked on water.

In our judgment this underscores the ambivalence and ambiguity of modernist theology. There is an intense concern to preserve theological continuity despite the extensive reconceptualizations of Christian categories. Thus, one finds many modernist clergy who have found a way to express faith in Jesus, but nonetheless have rejected the supernatural components of the Christology. Although we shall not utilize these items (in Table 3) in our Orthodoxy Index, we are inclined to accept the particular, rather than the general, as the better measure of theological convictions.

The central promise, and even premise, of the Christian tradition is everlasting life. As the Apostle Paul wrote: "If in this life only we have hope in Christ, we are of all men most miserable" (I Cor. 15:19). And as the late Episcopalian Bishop James A. Pike made clear, one need not even accept the existence of a personal God or the divinity of Christ to sustain Christian commitment to a life after death. This is, indeed, obvious in Table 4. While 67 per cent of the Protestant clergy were certain of the existence of God, and 61 per cent were certain of the divinity of Jesus, a higher proportion, 79 per cent, believed that the promise of "a life beyond death" is "literally true." This discrepancy becomes especially acute when one considers the second line in the table, belief in the Devil. Only 41 per cent of the Protestant clergy accepted the existence of a fiery fate beyond the grave, while nearly twice as many believed in a life after death. This could be called positive thinking. Not only do more clergy believe in life after death than believe in God or Christ, but a great many think life after death is an unmitigated blessing: without the possibility of Hell.

This tendency to positive thinking is mainly evident among the liberal denominations, those on the left of the table. The discrepancy between belief in a life after death and belief in the Devil is 60/8 for United Church of Christ clergy, 62/7 for Methodists, 77/23 for Episcopalians,

Table 4. LIFE AFTER DEATH; THE DEVIL

	United Church of Christ	Metho-dist	Epis-copal	Presby-terian	Luth. Church in Amer.	Amer. Luth. Church	American Baptist	Mis-souri Lutheran	South. Baptist	Total
"There is a life beyond death." Per cent who responded "Literally true"	60	62	77	77	84	93	93	97	99	79
"The Devil actually exists." Per cent who responded "Literally true"	8	7	23	26	43	75	66	93	94	41

and so on across the table until the Missouri Lutherans, where the contrast is a slight 97/93 and the Southern Baptists where it is 99/94. Clergy in denominations on the right of the table overwhelmingly accept the whole of the Christian tradition: a personal God, the divinity of Jesus, Christ's miracles, life after death, and the existence of the Devil. Those on the left of the table tend to reject these other tenets while still embracing the literal truth of life beyond death.

These patterns of belief among the clergy are virtually indistinguishable from those found previously among the laity. We must, therefore, reconfirm earlier judgments about the development of secularization and of a "New Denominationalism."[4]

Until quite recently it was commonly believed that American denominationalism was an organizational anachronism soon to be swept away by a rising tide of ecumenism. On all sides churchmen, journalists, and scholars were apparently convinced that, despite the lingering existence of several hundred separately constituted Christian bodies, the predominant fact about American religion was its unity of vision: that American Christians had come to share a "common-core" theological perspective.[5]

On reflection, it is now difficult to see how this misconception was sustained. The evidence of theological conflict was so obvious. On one side Christian scholars were engaged in a massive reexamination and demythologizing reinterpretation of Scripture, while in other sectors of Christianity, among the Southern Baptists, for example, seminary professors were being fired for questioning literal belief in the Book of Genesis. Presumably, the sudden spurt of denominational mergers caused a general inattention to theological disputes.

In any event, the earlier research on Christian laymen made it clear not only that denominationalism was still a major religious fact but also that, if anything, it was becoming more basic. In the past, theological conflict had occurred on many peripheral issues—infant versus adult baptism, for example—amid general agreement on the essential postulates of Christianity. The lay data indicated that these historic bases of religious dispute had, in fact, lost their original divisive force. But, concomitantly, a new and more basic set of divisions had come into being. These new fissures in the Christian community go to the very core of doctrine. Among laymen the new disputes are no longer over such matters as how to worship God properly, but whether or not there is a

God of the sort it makes any sense to worship at all; not over whether the bread and wine of communion became the actual body and blood of Christ through transubstantiation or are only symbolic, but whether or not Jesus was merely a man. These data forced the authors to the conclusion that at no previous time in history had denominationalism been supported by such widespread and important disputes. For example, while only 13 per cent of the United Church of Christ members and 21 per cent of the Methodists still confidently expect the Second Coming of Christ, three-quarters of the Missouri Synod Lutherans and 94 per cent of the Southern Baptist laity remain firmly committed to this major Christian doctrine. Differences such as these belie any conceivable form of theological unity among American Christians. Any apparent unity is superficial and tenuous.

At the time these findings were published some critics suggested that while diversity may be the primary feature of the beliefs held by Christian laity, differences were much less profound among the clergy. We, too, thought it entirely possible that interdenominational differences in theological convictions might be smaller among the clergy than among the laity, but we also felt that clerical differences would still be extensive. A subsequent study by Jeffrey K. Hadden showed that, in fact, differences among the clergy were virtually identical to those found among laymen.[6]

The data examined in this chapter fully confirm Hadden's findings. Tables showing that 8 per cent of clergy in one denomination hold a particular belief, while 98 per cent in another do so, approach maximum possible magnitude of disagreement. When responses to the same items by the clergy and the earlier samples of the laity are compared, they are found to be virtually identical.

The New Denominationalism encompasses the whole of the churches, both laity and clergy. The substance of theological divergence makes it seem likely that denominations may be headed for more intense conflicts, rather than moving forth in concert into an ecumenical age.

To ask how this new pattern of denominational conflict emerged raises the question of secularization. Obviously, interdenominational disagreements over fundamental Christian tenets exist to such a dramatic degree today because the overwhelming majority of ministers and members in some major denominations have rejected traditional doctrines in favor of a demythologized religious perspective, while in other denominations virtually everyone, members and clergy alike, has retained the "old-time religion" of his fathers and grandfathers. It has been widely recognized that religion has been undergoing secularization; that out of dissatisfaction with the inability of traditional doctrines and categories to comprehend and interpret the modern world at all adequately and to accommodate the burgeoning scientific revolution, there has been widespread theological reformulation.

But obviously this process has not occurred uniformly throughout Christianity. Instead it has been mainly concentrated in some of the denominations—where virtually everyone has been affected—while some other denominations have remained almost impervious. The result is the splintered Christian community witnessed in these survey findings. Consequently, all assertions about secularization must be properly qualified by reference to specific denominations: it is a major or minor phenomenon, depending on where one looks. And it has affected the clergy neither more nor less than the laity.

An Index of Orthodoxy[7]

In the preceding section we examined patterns of clergy belief on a variety of basic Christian tenets and found considerable variation. In order to proceed, it is necessary to construct a general summary measure of these variations: a way of classifying clergymen in terms of their commitment to Christian orthodoxy.

In the earlier study of the laity an Orthodoxy Index was constructed from four central Christian doctrines: the existence of a personal God, the divinity of Jesus Christ, the authenticity of Biblical miracles, and the existence of the Devil. In scoring this index a respondent received 1 point for each of these doctrines on which he expressed unwavering belief in the orthodox Christian position. On each item in response to which he acknowledged doubt or disbelief in the orthodox position, the respondent received no points. Thus an individual could score as high as 4 by reporting firm belief in all four doctrines or as low as zero by expressing doubt or disbelief in all four. In the present study we have followed the same procedure to classify clergymen according to their degree of orthodoxy.[8]

Repeating this technique, and, indeed, continuing to call the measure the Orthodoxy Index, flies in the face of a good deal of previous criticism.

Some critics protested the name we employed to describe it. More serious were vigorous criticisms of the index as inadequate to measure individual religious perspectives because the items from which it was constructed were too few and too crude. Since these criticisms have not persuaded us to modify our practices, it seems incumbent on us to explain why.

The use of the term "orthodoxy" to characterize an index of traditional religious belief is consistent with the standard dictionary definition of the term: "conforming to the Christian faith as formulated in the early ecumenical creeds and confessions." That is the reason it was used before and the reason we continue to do so. Judging by previous reactions to this usage, readers who accept the beliefs we have grouped under the name orthodoxy will find this quite acceptable. Such persons define themselves as orthodox believers, and our similar classification of them will be acceptable. Conflict arises with those who reject these beliefs (and a substantial number of both laymen and clergymen do) and by our procedure are hereby denied the label orthodox. Such persons, we suspect, would prefer to drop the word "orthodox" from the Christian vocabulary altogether. But if it is to be retained, they feel they also have a legitimate claim to the title, regardless of how they stand on traditional tenets of faith. There is a sense in which the word "orthodoxy" seems to hold latent implications of superiority: acceptance of the best or the truest or the most authentic theological views. Thus, those who reject traditional views also regard them as old-fashioned and narrow and object to their description as orthodoxy. Consequently, the authors of the earlier study have often been chastized for failing to measure true orthodoxy and for taking only an old-fashioned view of orthodoxy into account.

As sociologists, it is not and was not our intention to take a position on what Christian orthodoxy *ought* to be. The authors simply wanted an efficient way to distinguish those who tend to accept Christian beliefs as traditionally formulated from those who do not. Earlier, other possible names for the index were considered, among them fundamentalism and supernaturalism. Both of these, however, were much less suitable. They are loaded with unintended implications and could be interpreted as pejoratives.

As the matter was pursued, it was soon discovered that no name that is not a neologism can be attached to the index without offending at least those persons who score at one end of it; and a neologism would simply shelve the problem, not solve it. The concept of what it is that the index measures would still have to be defined and in a way that confronts the fact that all the component items are basic tenets of historic Christian doctrine. Orthodoxy is the term that best captures this specific meaning, so the decision was made to name the index accordingly rather than smuggle it into subsequent theorizing. In no way do we mean to denigrate the religious views of those who score low on the index; neither do we desire to take part in the argument as to which version of Christianity is the best theology. We simply want to capture variations in the degree to which Christian laymen and clergymen remain convinced of the truth of what, at least historically, has been regarded as the heart of Christian theology.

A more serious charge against the index has been that it is methodologically inadequate to serve these classificatory purposes. It has been vigorously argued that no theologically literate person could respond to our questions because they force a choice between both extreme and simple-minded positions. Furthermore, it is claimed, even when people do cooperate and choose an answer from the alternatives offered them, the results can only be a very distorted picture of their "true" theological position.

Now, it is evident that questions which are to be asked uniformly of people from all walks of life must be stated simply and clearly so that even the least educated and sophisticated among them can understand. Moreover, when respondents are required to choose from among pre-formulated answers, rather than give an open-ended or free response, the answer categories must be comprehensive so that people can find a suitable alternative. In extensively pretesting the questions, considerable pains were taken to ensure they were understandable and that the answer categories provided allowed respondents to find a suitable alternative. In the final version of the questionnaire they were also encouraged at a number of points along the way to skip a question if they found that none of the answer categories suited them. Furthermore, on a number of key questions respondents were also invited to reject the answer categories provided and to make up their own. As indicated earlier in this chapter, two of the four questions used in the Orthodoxy Index— these on belief in God and in the divinity of Jesus—took this form.

In the study of laymen less than half of 1 per cent rejected the answer categories provided on the questions about God and about Christ. As would be expected, more of the clergy did so: 9 per cent on the God question and 14 per cent on the question about Jesus. Nevertheless, the overwhelming majority of the clergy—91 per cent on the God question and 86 per cent on the Jesus question—felt comfortable using an answer category provided by the authors. Furthermore, as we have mentioned earlier, an examination of the answers written in by those who utilized this opportunity did not reveal new categories which needed to be added to the questions. Most could have been legitimately recoded into one of the existing response categories. In order to avoid disputes that such recoding had produced our findings, we retained all write-in answers unchanged.

The fact that laymen demonstrated little discomfort with the available answer categories did not persuade the critics that the items were suitable. But now we see that the clergy, too, were overwhelmingly content to register their theological beliefs within our "simple-minded" alternatives. To continue to believe that theologically literate persons could not use these categories is to imply either that the vast majority of Protestant clergy are theological illiterates or that they care so little about registering their true beliefs that they will not bother to write them in. Whatever the case may be, we are concerned with studying the churches as they are, and, to this end, our items would appear to have proved their adequacy.

These findings, of course, do not establish the validity of the index: Does it reliably measure what it is supposed to measure? Nor do they answer the charge that the index fails to register the modernist alternatives to traditional Christian theology.

It was not the authors' goal in previous studies, nor is it in this one, to use the Orthodoxy Index to comprehend all the variations and subtle distinctions in Christian doctrine. The index was developed to test the proposition that unwavering commitment to traditional Christian dogma was the first link in a causal chain leading to anti-Semitism. We require the index to identify respondents validly according to the degree to which they retain such commitment. As it happens, the Orthodoxy Index is a considerably more comprehensive and sensitive measure than it appears to be. Before reporting evidence on this, however, let us examine how reliably it does the more limited task for which it was designed.

In *Christian Beliefs and Anti-Semitism*[9] and again in *American Piety*,[10] it was shown that for Christian laymen the Orthodoxy Index strongly predicted other beliefs not included in the index. That is, the higher a person's score on the index, the greater the probability he would unequivocally hold other central tenets of Christian teachings. Thus it was clear that including a greater number of items in the index would not importantly increase its precision.[11]

Following this same logic, Table 5 reveals that among Protestant ministers also the Orthodoxy Index accurately reflects other beliefs not included in it. For example, *not a single* clergyman with a zero score on the index expressed literal belief in the Virgin Birth, while 97 per cent of those with scores of 4 on the index did so. Similarly, none of those who scored zero on orthodoxy believed Jesus literally walked on water, whereas 95 per cent of the highest scorers did so. Finally, the table shows that while none of the zero scorers and only 4 per cent of those with scores of 1 on the Orthodoxy Index held a literal or nearly literal interpretation of the Bible, nearly three-quarters of the highest scorers did so. This last relationship is even more powerful than it appears at first glance. Of the

Table 5.   THE RELATIONSHIP BETWEEN ORTHODOXY AND OTHER RELIGIOUS
BELIEFS AMONG PROTESTANT MINISTERS

	Orthodoxy Index				
	Low				High
	0	1	2	3	4
Number	(193)	(246)	(209)	(292)	(584)
Per cent who believe it is "Literally true" that "Jesus was born of a virgin."	0	13	23	44	97
Per cent who believe it is "Literally true" that "Jesus walked on water."	0	10	23	43	95
Per cent who "strongly agree" or "agree" with the statement: "I believe in a literal or nearly literal interpretation of the Bible."	0	4	10	11	74

212 ministers who said they "strongly" agreed with the statement, 202 had maximum scores of 4 on the Orthodoxy Index. As survey data go, this is remarkable consistency and reveals that the index does, indeed, distinguish clergymen who are more committed to traditional Christian doctrines from those who are less so.

Thus it seems clear that the index is adequate to the tasks for which it was created. But we believe that, in fact, it does more than that. We have evidence that it quite accurately characterizes in a more holistic way the general theological orientations of the clergy: explicitly, their theological self-conceptions.

Because ministers are religious professionals, seminary-trained in religious discourse and, necessarily, theologically self-conscious, it was possible to ask them to appraise their own theological views in a way not possible in the earlier surveys of laymen. In contemporary theological discussions four main categories have been developed to characterize conflicting points of view. These are Fundamentalist, Conservative, Neo-orthodox, and Liberal. These terms are widely used, and their meaning is generally understood and agreed upon by religious professionals.

Admittedly, there is considerable variation of viewpoint among those who share any one of these general labels; yet they have been found suitable for continued and constant use in theology, and, more importantly, most clergymen define themselves theologically in terms of one of these labels. We have taken advantage of the existence of this categorization of theological self-conceptions among religious professionals to assess the validity of the Orthodoxy Index. How much agreement is there between the characterization of a clergyman's religious perspective on the basis of the index and his own characterization of himself?

As can be seen in Table 6, the extent of agreement is considerable. For example, not a single minister with a score of 2 or less on the Orthodoxy Index identified himself as a Fundamentalist, while 1 per cent of those who scored 3 did so and 15 per cent of those with a maximum score of 4 did so. Read the other way, of 89 ministers who regarded themselves as Fundamentalists, 86 scored 4 on the Orthodoxy Index and the other 3 scored 3. This same close agreement between self-conception and index score continues down the table. While 3 per cent of those with zero scores on the index thought of themselves as Conservatives, 30 per cent of those who scored 3 and 70 per cent of

Table 6. ORTHODOXY AND MINISTERS' THEOLOGICAL SELF-CONCEPTION

	Orthodoxy Index				
	Low				High
	0	1	2	3	4
Number	(193)	(246)	(209)	(292)	(584)
"Admittedly, there are difficulties associated with describing oneself in terms of broad theological positions. However, within the following categories, which of the following best describes your theological position?"					
Per cent:					
Fundamentalist	0	0	0	1	15
Conservative	3	7	16	30	70
Neo-orthodox	20	26	28	27	7
Liberal	61	54	46	30	3
Other	16	12	10	12	5
No answer	0	1	0	0	0
	100%	100%	100%	100%	100%

those who scored 4 did so. Thus, 85 per cent of those with maximum scores of 4 on the index reported that their theological self-conception was Fundamentalist or Conservative. Similarly, 61 per cent of those who scored zero on the index described themselves as Liberals, while only 3 per cent of those who scored 4 did so.

From these findings it is evident that the Orthodoxy Index affords a classification of the clergy's theological position which is highly consistent with their self-conceptions. Indeed, for these clergy, the concordance is so great that these two measures ought to be empirically interchangeable: the findings produced by one measure ought to be virtually identical with those produced by the other.

Table 7 demonstrates this interchangeability. The first line in the table characterizes denominations by the proportion of their clergy who scored high (4) on the Orthodoxy Index. The second row depicts denominations by the proportion of clergy who classified themselves theologically as Fundamentalists or Conservatives. The findings are in virtually total agreement. Any conclusions one might draw on the extent of doc-

Table 7. COMPARISON OF DENOMINATIONAL PROFILES BASED ON ORTHODOXY INDEX SCORES OF CLERGY AND ON THE THEOLOGICAL SELF-IMAGE OF THE CLERGY

Response Category	United Church of Christ	Methodist	Episcopal	Presbyterian	Luth. Church in Amer.	Amer. Luth. Church	American Baptist	Missouri Lutheran	South. Baptist
Per cent high (4) on Orthodoxy Index[a]	7	6	19	24	39	59	65	89	95
Number	(133)	(333)	(196)	(220)	(85)	(117)	(143)	(130)	(167)
Per cent who classified themselves theologically as "Fundamentalist" or "Conservative"[b]	8	9	25	36	34	68	67	87	95
Number	(137)	(350)	(204)	(225)	(86)	(115)	(144)	(131)	(167)

[a] Percentages based only on those who answered all questions making up Orthodoxy Index.
[b] Percentages based only on those who answered the question.

trinal disunity among Protestant denominations or the relative position of a denomination would not be importantly affected by using one measure rather than the other.[12]

Particularism

"Christians do believe that all Jews who reject Christ as the Messiah are therefore lost from God's redeeming love—as are all men of all races who have not personally responded to God's grace through faith in Jesus Christ. This is not racism; this is the Christian doctrine of personal salvation."

—WAYNE DEHONEY,
President, Southern Baptist Convention.
Letter to the Editors of *Newsweek*,
May 23, 1966, in response to a story
on *Christian Beliefs and Anti-Semitism*.

In the earlier work it was argued—and the authors tried to demonstrate—that certain kinds of theologies imply a narrow and precisely defined sphere of persons who qualify as properly religious. Such conceptions of proper religious status, tantamount to religious chauvinism, were identified as religious *particularism*.

Most simply, religious particularism is the belief that only one's own religion is legitimate and that all others are necessarily false, impotent, and perhaps even wicked. While particularism was initially developed to refer to a general phenomenon found in a number of religions, our primary interest was in its Christian manifestations. As is recognized by *Webster's New World Dictionary*, which defines particularism as "the theological doctrine that redemption is possible only for certain individuals," the primary issue in Christian particularism concerns salvation: Who are viewed as eligible or ineligible for entrance to God's Kingdom? Specifically, are all followers of non-Christian faiths automatically damned? The historic Christian answer has been "yes." Indeed, for centuries not only did Christians hold that non-Christians were unredeemed, but various Christian bodies even denied the possibility of salvation for followers of competing Christian groups.

The importance of particularism for our analysis seems fairly obvious. Clearly it cannot be construed as racism directly. President Dehoney of the Southern Baptist Convention misunderstood the earlier work in making that assertion. What is important is that Christian commitment to the doctrine that all "who have not personally responded to God's grace through faith in Jesus Christ" are "therefore lost" means that non-Christians are stigmatized as "damned." Furthermore, while those who are committed to Christian particularism also thereby condemn Moslems, Buddhists, and followers of other religions, in our society such judgments fall almost entirely on Jews, for they are the only highly visible non-Christians in our midst.[13]

Again, this in itself is not directly racist,[14] but it does provide a basis for prejudice. As we shall argue in subsequent chapters, it is easy to accept negative beliefs about those whom one already defines negatively. It is only a short step from religious hostility to anti-Semitism. When one already believes that Jews, for some perverse reason, reject salvation through Christ and are damned, it seems plausible that they should also cheat and connive. But we are getting ahead of ourselves.

In recent times many theologians have rejected the historic doctrine that salvation comes only through Christ. The Catholic Church has for decades promulgated the doctrine of the unconscious Catholic, which states that anyone who sincerely seeks religious truth and is honestly committed to whatever he believes to be religious truth is seeking Catholicism, but has failed to find it, and is thus both unconsciously a Catholic and one of the saved. This may be a convoluted argument, but its implications are profound, for it opens salvation to all religions. Indeed, in the earlier study distinct evidence was uncovered that this doctrine had made American Catholics more resistant than their Protestant counterparts to linking religious beliefs and anti-Semitism. Similarly, many Protestant theologians and spokesmen now reject the idea of automatic damnation for non-Christians. Nevertheless, the majority of Christian laymen still retained the belief that only those who accepted Christ could be saved, and this made an important difference in their response to Jews.

Table 8 shows that the earlier findings did not reflect a cultural lag between the clergy and the laity: 69 per cent of the Protestant clergy in our sample responded that "Belief in Jesus Christ as Saviour" is "*absolutely* necessary" for "Salvation" (and 65 per cent of Protestant laymen gave this response). Over all, the data confirm President Dehoney's claim that most Christians, both laymen and clergy, do believe redemption is possible only through acceptance of Christ.

However, as with the other doctrines examined earlier in this chap-

Table 8. DENOMINATION AND PARTICULARISM

(Per cent who responded that "Belief in Jesus Christ as Saviour" is "Absolutely Necessary" for "Salvation.")

	United Church of Christ	Metho-dist	Epis-copal	Presby-terian	Luth. Church in Amer.	Amer. Luth. Church	American Baptist	Mis-souri Lutheran	South. Baptist	Total
Per cent	29	46	56	74	78	88	90	97	99	69
Number	(137)	(354)	(207)	(226)	(87)	(118)	(147)	(134)	(170)	(1,580)

ter, the "Total" figure is something of a statistical fiction: most real denominations differ rather sharply from the findings for "all Protestants." Only a small minority of United Church of Christ clergy (29 per cent) have a particularistic commitment, as do 46 per cent of the Methodists and 56 per cent of the Episcopalians. On the other side of the table, 90 per cent of the American Baptists, 97 per cent of the Missouri Synod Lutherans, and 99 per cent of the Southern Baptists reject the possibility of salvation for persons who do not accept Jesus as the Saviour. From what we have already seen of the distribution of orthodoxy among the denominations, these differences imply that particularism is mainly associated with orthodoxy.

In the previous study the authors sought to explain how traditional Christian orthodoxy leads to a particularistic conception of religious authenticity. We shall not repeat that analysis here. Suffice it to say that Table 9 clearly demonstrates the strong relationship between the Orthodoxy Index and the propensity to regard belief in Jesus as "absolutely necessary" for salvation. While 23 per cent of the ministers scoring zero on orthodoxy gave this response, 97 per cent of those who scored 4 did so.

Table 9. ORTHODOXY AND PARTICULARISM

	Orthodoxy Index				
	Low				High
	0	1	2	3	4
Number	(193)	(246)	(209)	(292)	(584)
Per cent who said "Belief in Jesus Christ as Saviour" is "Absolutely Necessary" for "Salvation."	23	45	58	76	97

To summarize our findings in this chapter: the data show that although there is great variation in the extent to which Protestant clergy hold the tenets of Christian orthodoxy, the *modal* clergyman retains a pristine orthodoxy and also rejects the possibility of salvation outside Christ. Thus, the first two steps in our explanatory scheme, orthodoxy and particularism, are just as evident among the clergy as they were found to be among church-members and are interrelated in a similar highly consistent fashion. Consequently, we have so far found no basis to suggest that enlarging our conception of "the churches" to include the clergy requires a revision of the earlier position. Of course, this is only the beginning of the analysis. Perhaps the clergy differ greatly from laymen when it comes to a specific confrontation of the Jewish question.

3

Religious Conceptions of the Jews

This chapter moves from general features of Christian doctrine to those components of Scripture and tradition which explicitly affect the Jews. First we shall assess briefly what the Protestant clergy believe about the role of the Jews in the Crucifixion. Then we shall examine their religious evaluations of the modern Jew: Do ministers in the latter half of the twentieth century judge their Jewish contemporaries guilty of the crime of deicide? Finally, we shall assemble the first four steps in our explanation (Orthodoxy→Particularism→Hostile Religious Image of the Historic Jew→Religious Hostility toward the Contemporary Jew) and evaluate its applicability and validity for the clergy.

The Crucifixion

The critical issue which has poisoned Christian-Jewish relations for two millenniums is: What collective role, if any, did the Jews play in the Crucifixion, and why? Despite a conciliatory voice raised now and then by Christian churchmen through the centuries, Christians have believed and taught that the Jews, as a people, bore sole responsibility for deicide.

Recently, however, in the lingering aftermath of the destruction of European Jewry many of the churches have recanted this view. While the earlier study was being completed the Roman Catholic Church, through Vatican Council II, denounced the doctrine of Jewish guilt for the Crucifixion. Although the statement eventually adopted by the church fathers was much less forceful than the preliminary version which had been approved, it was nevertheless sufficient to provide the mass of clergy with a theological basis from which to attack the notion of Jewish guilt.[1] Furthermore, while the Catholic action received a great deal of press attention, most Protestant bodies had formally adopted such a position somewhat earlier and often more vigorously. Today, only a few denominations—for instance, the Missouri Synod Lutherans and the Southern Baptists—have failed to denounce the pernicious doctrine of Jewish guilt in unequivocal terms.

However, official church actions can hardly be expected to change people's minds overnight. Indeed, research has shown that, more often than not, Protestants remain completely unaware of the various official pronouncements of their denominations,[2] and recent reactions to the Pope's reaffirmation of the ban on artificial means of contraception hardly indicate that compliance among Catholics is automatic either. Still, one might expect the clergy to be relatively more responsive to doctrinal changes, especially those concerning the Jewish role in the Crucifixion, for this belief seems to have been long outmoded and was always "bad" theology anyway.

If Christ's death and the suffering on the cross were necessary to atone for our sins, the instrument of His death must be the sinfulness of mankind. The guilt as well as the blessing must be universal. Would there have been no Crucifixion if the Jewish elders had not desired the death of Jesus? The line of reasoning that begins with blaming the Jews for the Crucifixion necessarily leads to absurdity, such as that spoken to a Jewish sutler by Union Army General Ebenezer Dumont: "If it hadn't been for just such damned cusses as you, our Lord Jesus Christ would be alive and well to this day."

The primary source for the threadbare epithet "Christ-killer" is the Book of Matthew, Chapter 27. Here we are told that Jesus was seized on complaints by the chief priests and elders and taken before Pontius Pilate, the Roman Procurator of Judea, for judgment. The chief priests and elders informed Pilate that Jesus claimed to be King of the Jews, a charge tantamount to treason under both Roman and Jewish law. But, Matthew goes on to tell us, Pilate felt sympathetic toward Jesus and realized that the priests were persecuting Jesus out of envy. Pilate's wife, because she had dreamed he ought to have nothing to do with the whole affair, further encouraged him to release Jesus.

Pilate attempted such a release by taking advantage of a custom by which a condemned prisoner was pardoned at feast time. He gave the multitude a choice between Jesus and one Barabbas, accused of murder and sedition.

This attempt was frustrated, Matthew charges, because the priests and elders persuaded the people to ask for the release of Barabbas. Thus forestalled, Pilate is reported to have protested that Jesus had done nothing. But he was drowned out by the multitude who shouted, "Let him be crucified!" Fearing tumult, Pilate is portrayed as backing down, and, calling for water, washing his hands before the mob to make clear his refusal to take responsibility for the blood of Jesus.

At this, Matthew reports, the people cried out, "His blood be on us, and on our children." Thus the Jewish throng is shown to call down a blood curse of eternal guilt upon themselves and future generations of the Jewish people.

In spite of the testimony contained in the Gospel and centuries of Christian presumption of Jewish guilt, we expect that the majority of the clergy no longer accept this position, although a majority of laymen still retain such views (58 per cent of the Protestants and 61 per cent of the Roman Catholics—see Chapter 1 for a more thorough discussion of findings among the laity).

On the other hand, we do not expect clergymen who hold such views to be a rarity, unless, of course, the critics are correct in positing that such beliefs stem from the general culture and not from religious institutions.

As can be seen in Table 10, while the majority of Protestant clergymen did not choose the Jews as the "group . . . most responsible for crucifying Christ," those who did so constitute a significant minority. One-third of the clergy do, in fact, still blame the Jews, despite official church pronouncements to the contrary. Placing blame for the Crucifixion on all of mankind is the position adopted by the majority; over all, 54 per cent of the clergy supported this view. The remainder were scattered: 7 per cent blamed the Romans, 1 per cent the Christians, and 4 per cent said they didn't know.

So, for every five clergymen who believe the guilt of the Crucifixion is universal, there are still three who blame the Jews. More importantly,

Table 10. DENOMINATION AND BLAME FOR THE CRUCIFIXION

Reply to: "Which group do you think was most responsible for crucifying Christ?"

Response Category	United Church of Christ	Methodist	Episcopal	Presbyterian	Luth. Church in Amer.	Amer. Luth. Church	American Baptist	Missouri Lutheran	South. Baptist	Total
Number	(137)	(354)	(207)	(226)	(87)	(118)	(147)	(134)	(170)	(1,580)
Jews	31%	35%	29%	36%	17%	31%	42%	22%	35%	32%
Romans	10	15	9	9	6	2	4	1	4	7
Christians	2	2	0	0	1	0	1	0	0	1
Mankind	45	43	55	50	69	65	48	73	59	54
Don't know	9	3	5	4	7	2	3	1	0	4
No answer	3	2	2	2	0	0	2	3	2	2
	100%	100%	100%	101%[a]	100%	100%	100%	100%	100%	100%

[a] Percentage does not add to 100 because of rounding error.

belief in Jewish guilt for the Crucifixion is not concentrated solely in those denominations which have not officially rejected this doctrine. Instead, clergy holding this view are relatively evenly spread among all the Protestant bodies: they are least common in the Lutheran Church in America (17 per cent) and most common in the American Baptist Convention (42 per cent). From this lack of any consistent denominational differences, it is obvious that belief in historic Jewish guilt is not a consequence of holding highly orthodox theological convictions. And, indeed, our analysis found that there was only a modest correlation between the two. Furthermore, belief in historic Jewish guilt was only modestly related to particularism. This is no surprise, for, as we shall see, belief in historic Jewish guilt may or may not have ramifications for conceptions of the modern Jew. Holding this historic image merely facilitates, but does not necessarily lead to, hostile religious images of Jews today. It is the latter which now concerns us.

Hostile Religious Conceptions of the Modern Jew

Although we have just seen that about a third of the Protestant clergy still cling to the notion of historic Jewish guilt for the Crucifixion, it does not necessarily follow that this has any bearing on their judgments about contemporary Jews. Such a belief could simply be held in a purely historical perspective and have no connotations for persons now living. Thus, for example, knowledge of Roman atrocities has no bearing on current beliefs about Italians, nor do we hold today's Scandinavians collectively responsible for the excesses perpetrated by Viking raiders. On the other hand, the Gospel account of the Crucifixion in Matthew contains the line "His blood be on us, and on our children." The Bible thereby provides a doctrinal basis for regarding the contemporary Jew, unlike Italians or Scandinavians, as tainted by the actions of long-dead ancestors. For centuries this linkage of living Jews with the "crime" of their forefathers dominated Christian attitudes and actions toward Jews —"Death to the Christ-killers" has long served as the call to pogrom.

When the initial study was undertaken it seemed unlikely that images of the contemporary Jews as Christ-killers, still suffering God's wrath, would find any substantial support among American Christians. It was recognized that such imagery was the common currency of the "lunatic fringe" hate merchants, some of whom have subsequently written the authors to reavow their doctrines; but there were few clues that such beliefs retained any appreciable appeal. The authors were surprised and depressed to find they had underestimated the stubborn persistence of such doctrines. In fact, a substantial minority of Christian laymen still viewed their Jewish neighbors as continuing to bear the alleged guilt of their forefathers for the Crucifixion of Christ and as still subject to God's punishment for this "historic" act. Many Christians were uncertain whether or not these beliefs are true, leaving only a minority who unequivocally rejected such beliefs as false. Even the horror of the Nazi era had not shaken these threadbare charges out of the Christian consciousness. They remained, a shabby deformity of the Christian conscience.

These particular findings of the earlier inquiry produced widespread denial that the churches had ever taught that Jews are damned or guilty of the Crucifixion or, at least, denial that such doctrines have been taught in recent times. These critics accepted the empirical evidence that many church members do hold such beliefs, but argued that since they can't be learning them in church, the church is not responsible and study should turn elsewhere. Indeed, according to a number of participants, a serious objection raised by conservative bishops during the Vatican Council against passing a statement absolving the Jews was that such doctrines had never been taught by the church and to pass a statement now would make it seem as if the church had been guilty of such teachings in the past! No fair reading of history could possibly result in an acceptance of the notion that the churches have never taken such positions on Jews. On the contrary, a surfeit of examples culled from Sunday school and parochial school texts show that such teaching was widespread until the last several years;[3] furthermore, not all of this material has yet been removed. Even more telling is the indisputable fact that such religious beliefs about Jews are more prevalent among the more orthodox and most devout members. This being the case, it seems highly unlikely that the churches have no part in continued promulgation of these beliefs.

Nevertheless, it is possible to argue, as some of the critics did, that the churches are only one among many sources of individual religiousness and religious beliefs. Much religion is learned at home and from the culture generally, and religious people could be absorbing religious ideas about Jews which, though originally implanted in the culture via church doctrines, are now sustained without any actual encouragement on the part of the churches. In this view an important source of anti-Semitism could well be religious beliefs, but beliefs which are in no way connected with the institutions of the churches.

In reply it must be acknowledged that the necessary resources or interest were not available to study in a systematic way the content of sermons, of Sunday school sessions, or of texts and tracts to determine whether or not the churches are the source of the religious images of Jews identified as being critical in producing anti-Semitism. The authors could only argue inferentially—from the existence of such beliefs among the laity and from the correlations between such beliefs and various forms of religious commitment and participation—that such must be the case. This argument is not conclusive.

The present study, however, allows a reassessment of the situation on the basis of systematic evidence. If there is significant sentiment among the clergy that the modern Jews are tainted by guilt for Christ's suffering and death, there is much less leeway to dismiss the findings among the laity as simply inauthentic Christianity which is in no way fostered by Christian institutions. The clergy may not be "the churches," but they would be the last to deny that they are the spokesmen of church teachings.

Finally, we expect that the processes leading from orthodoxy and particularism combined with reverence for other historic Christian doctrines—including those concerning Jews—operate among the clergy as among the laity. For what has been advanced is essentially a cognitive chain: given certain belief premises, certain conclusions about the religious status of modern Jewry logically follow. Since, as we have already seen, the premises are held by the clergy as well as the laity, it is likely that the conclusions drawn by the clergy will to some extent be the same as those found among the laity. Now we shall see.

Ministers were asked (as were laymen before them) to agree or disagree with the statement, "The Jews can never be forgiven for what they did to Jesus until they accept Him as the True Saviour" (see Table 11). This statement summarizes much of the traditional Christian hostility toward Jews. "What they did to Jesus" was, of course, to reject and crucify Him; that the Jews "can never be forgiven" indicates that they remain unabsolved, and the price of salvation is to stop rejecting Jesus and become Christians. It is not the case, as no one would ever have predicted, that the majority of Protestant clergy agreed with this statement (19 per cent did). But neither did the majority reject it outright; less than half (48 per cent) said they "strongly disagree" with this statement. In our judgment the item is not very subtle, but promulgates an invidious religious condemnation of Jewry—a condemnation that has itself clearly been officially dismissed by nearly all Christian bodies. It is true that an additional 27 per cent of the clergy were willing to "disagree" with the statement, and thus it can be claimed that 75 per cent disagree to some extent. However, careful study of the data indicates that there is a meaningful difference between "strongly disagree" and simply "disagree," and that discrepancy reflects a qualitative difference in opposition to this charge against the Jews. Looking at denominational contrasts, it becomes clear that unwillingness to select "strongly disagree" rather than just "disagree," and willingness to in fact "agree" or even "strongly agree" with the item, follow a highly consistent pattern: Southern Baptists were reluctant to either "strongly disagree" or "disagree" (only 22 per cent), while United Church of Christ clergy were likely to do one or the other (94 per cent did).

This raises the matter of denominational differences. Here, as on orthodoxy and particularism, the extent of denominational contrast is huge. Thus, while 73 per cent of the United Church of Christ clergy, 67 per cent of the Episcopalians, and 64 per cent of the Methodists strongly disagreed with the item, only 28 per cent of the ministers of the American Lutheran Church, 15 per cent of the Missouri Lutherans, and 11 per cent of the Southern Baptists strongly disagreed. Conversely, while *not a single* United Church of Christ pastor, and only 1 per cent of the Methodists, Presbyterians, and Lutheran Church in America clergy *strongly agreed* with the item, a quarter of the Missouri Lutherans and nearly half (45 per cent) of the Southern Baptists strongly agreed. Indeed, adding "strongly agree" and "agree," we find more than half of the Missouri Lutheran clergy and more than two-thirds of the Southern Baptists accept the truth of the notion that the Jews cannot be forgiven for the Crucifixion, short of conversion. Southern Baptists were four times more likely to "strongly agree" than they were to "strongly disagree."

From this table we must conclude that the image of the Jews as still guilty of the Crucifixion and unredeemed is far from dead among the

Table 11. DENOMINATION AND "THE JEWS CAN NEVER BE FORGIVEN FOR WHAT THEY DID TO JESUS UNTIL THEY ACCEPT HIM AS THE TRUE SAVIOUR."

Response Category	United Church of Christ	Metho-dist	Epis-copal	Presby-terian	Luth. Church in Amer.	Amer. Luth. Church	American Baptist	Mis-souri Lutheran	South. Baptist	Total
"Strongly disagree"	73%	64%	67%	51%	59%	28%	32%	15%	11%	48%
"Disagree"	21	30	26	36	30	31	30	24	11	27
"No opinion"	2	3	4	8	3	10	7	8	9	6
"Agree"	4	2	1	4	7	21	19	28	24	10
"Strongly agree"	0	1	2	1	1	10	12	25	45	9
Per cent	100	100	100	100	100	100	100	100	100	100
Number[a]	(136)	(351)	(203)	(217)	(81)	(109)	(140)	(113)	(156)	(1,506)

[a] Table based only on those ministers who answered the item.

Protestant clergy. A majority will not strongly reject it; one in five will actively advocate it; and in some denominations acceptance far exceeds rejection.

Table 12 presents clergy beliefs on a much more invidious conception of the modern Jew: as cursed by God. The clergy, again like the laity before them, were asked to respond to the statement: "The reason the Jews have so much trouble is because God is punishing them for rejecting Jesus."

This item gets to the heart of the legacy of the Matthew story—"His blood be on us." It places the responsibility for their centuries of persecution and tribulation on the Jews themselves. Indeed, it seems to justify persecution and hatred of Jews as divinely ordained—a kind of heaven-sent anti-Semitism.

As would be expected, the data show that the idea of God-sent persecution of the Jews is not widespread among the clergy and is considerably less common than the notion that the Jews remain unforgiven for the Crucifixion. Over all, only 8 per cent of the clergy agreed or strongly agreed with the statement (11 per cent of the laymen agreed). Considering the content of the item, it is hardly unimportant that approximately 124 of 1,555 clergymen hold such a position. On the other hand, about ten times as many of them (88 per cent) disagreed or strongly disagreed with the item. This picture of overwhelming disagreement must, however, be qualified on two counts: the degree of disagreement and denominational contrasts.

A considerably less than overwhelming 61 per cent of the clergy strongly disagreed with the statement. Furthermore, denominational differences strongly suggest once again that there is an important difference between strongly disagreeing and merely disagreeing: the proportion of clergy who simply disagree increases in denominations where agreement is also higher. Thus, among clergy of the United Church of Christ, 79 per cent strongly disagreed and another 15 per cent disagreed, while only 2 per cent agreed. Among Southern Baptists only 27 per cent strongly disagreed, while 36 per cent disagreed and 26 per cent agreed.

We have seen that these two hostile religious conceptions of modern Jewry are not a purely lay phenomenon. The clergy are nearly as likely as the laity to hold them. Such beliefs persist in all denominations, and in some they can hardly be seen as a residue of things past, for they are

Table 12. DENOMINATION AND "THE REASON THE JEWS HAVE SO MUCH TROUBLE IS BECAUSE GOD IS PUNISHING THEM FOR REJECTING JESUS."

Response Category	United Church of Christ	Metho-dist	Epis-copal	Presby-terian	Luth. Church in Amer.	Amer. Luth. Church	American Baptist	Mis-souri Lutheran	South. Baptist	Total
"Strongly disagree"	79%	78%	79%	68%	63%	37%	47%	28%	27%	61%
"Disagree"	15	18	19	26	26	46	31	44	36	27
"No opinion"	4	2	1	2	7	7	4	10	11	4
"Agree"	2	2	1	3	4	10	14	15	17	6
"Strongly agree"	0	0	0	1	0	0	4	3	9	2
Per cent	100	100	100	100	100	100	100	100	100	100
Number[a]	(136)	(352)	(206)	(220)	(86)	(117)	(145)	(129)	(164)	(1,555)

[a] Table based on only those ministers who answered the item.

held by a majority or a large minority of the clergy.

These findings hardly support the claim that the churches bear no responsibility for the persistence of such conceptions among contemporary Christians and that church members must learn this part of their religion elsewhere, certainly not in church. The patterns of clergy and lay response to these questions are so tediously similar that they suggest that it is precisely in church and Sunday school that the learning takes place.

We suspect that these findings will disturb serious Christians as much as if not more than the earlier results for laymen did, for they are also more disturbing to us, as we shall discuss in Chapters 4 and 5. And yet they are not surprising. Considering the explanation developed in the earlier study of why Christians take these hostile positions vis-à-vis the contemporary Jew, there was no basis for supposing that the clergy would be doing much better than the laity.

It was argued that such beliefs are intrinsic to historic Christian doctrine and that their survival should mainly be a product of the continuance of traditional Christian orthodoxy. Obviously such orthodoxy is not a purely lay phenomenon; our data have shown that it is not. Consequently, one would expect some of the clergy to hold hostile religious conceptions of Jews.

This was confirmed by our analysis, which showed that responses on each of the religious hostility items was strongly predicted by scores on the Orthodoxy Index. However, a proper assessment, as well as further analysis, depends on merging both items into a single measure, subject to simultaneous analysis—as was done with religious beliefs through the Orthodoxy Index.

Thus, responses to these two items (Tables 11 and 12) were systematically scored to produce an Index of Religious Hostility toward Contemporary Jews, hereafter called the Religious Hostility Index. Questions of validity have previously been well covered in *Christian Beliefs and Anti-Semitism* and are identical with those confronted earlier in respect of the Orthodoxy Index, with one major exception: while many will always argue over who deserves the title "orthodox," we expect few will disagree with the construction we have put on the face meaning of these items referring to the religious status of the contemporary Jew. Granted some will argue that these items simply represent Christian truth and that, far from being hostile, they only reflect their intense desire to bring the Jews into the Christian community. But even then, few would deny that such items connote a basic antipathy toward those Jews who refuse conversion and actively prefer to remain "unredeemed." And this, of course, has been the real problem for nearly two millenniums. The Reverend Richard John Neuhaus, in a *Una Sancta* editorial condemning church reactions to the earlier findings, has put it well:

> "We just want to save all those poor Jews from going to hell! That's not anti-Semitism; it's Christian love." Thus spake the king of Spain when, at sword point, he gave the Jews the choice of conversion or worse. The Glock-Stark study has been criticized for referring to Luther's anti-Semitism (*Dialog*), about which the less said the better. In defense of Luther, it has been asserted (*Lutheran Witness Reporter,* June 19) that his remarks about the Jews must be understood in the light of his bitter disappointment at their unwillingness to be converted to a reformed Christianity. Surely, if Luther must be defended, a more adequate case should be developed. Is it not anti-Semitism to say to the Jew, "I'll accept you if you agree to become like me"?

In our own minds there is no ambiguity over the essentially hostile nature of these two items. They blame contemporary Jews for the Crucifixion and charge that Jews continue to suffer God's wrath and unforgiveness as a result. Scoring each item in a systematic way, we are able to examine their cumulative effect, in Table 13.[4]

Over all, 45 per cent of the clergy scored zero on the Religious Hostility Index (strongly disagreed with both items), and the table shows that the Protestant denominations differ greatly on this criterion, the proportions falling sharply from left to right. On the one hand, 71 per cent of United Church of Christ clergy, two-thirds of the Episcopalians (66 per cent), and 62 per cent of the Methodists scored zero, while only 24 per cent of the American Baptist clergy, 18 per cent of the American Lutheran Church, 11 per cent of the Missouri Lutherans, and a tiny 7 per cent of the Southern Baptists vigorously rejected both of these extreme statements about modern Jews. Southern Baptists were more than six times as likely to score high, indicating some sympathy for both statements, than they were to score zero; among Missouri Lutherans the ratio was more than three to one. Indeed, 79 per cent of Southern Baptists and 60 per cent of Missouri Lutherans as compared with 5 per cent of Methodists and 6 per cent of Episcopalians, scored medium or high on the Religious Hostility Index.

Table 13. DENOMINATION AND RELIGIOUS HOSTILITY TOWARD CONTEMPORARY JEWS

Religious Hostility Index:	United Church of Christ	Metho-dist	Epis-copal	Presby-terian	Luth. Church in Amer.	Amer. Luth. Church	American Baptist	Mis-souri Lutheran	South. Baptist	Total
Zero	71%	62%	66%	48%	50%	18%	24%	11%	7%	45%
Low	22	33	28	41	37	39	35	29	14	31
Medium	5	3	5	8	7	30	25	25	35	13
High	2	2	1	3	6	13	16	35	44	11
Per cent	100	100	100	100	100	100	100	100	100	100
Number[a]	(136)	(350)	(203)	(216)	(81)	(108)	(139)	(113)	(154)	(1,500)

[a] Table based only on those ministers who answered both items making up the index.

Given these profound denominational differences, the pattern which emerges in Table 14 is no surprise. Here we see that orthodoxy strongly influences religious hostility. While 75 per cent of those who scored zero on orthodoxy also scored zero on religious hostility and none scored high, only 16 per cent of those who scored 4 (maximum) on orthodoxy scored zero on religious hostility, while 29 per cent scored high.

Closer examination of the data in Table 14 reveals that while the effect of orthodoxy is systematic, there is a marked difference between the extent of religious hostility displayed by those with scores of 3 and those scoring 4 on orthodoxy. Thus, while 50 per cent of those scoring 3 on orthodoxy scored zero on religious hostility, only 16 per cent of those scoring 4 did so, and while only 3 per cent of those scoring 3 on orthodoxy scored high on hostility, 29 per cent of those scoring 4 did so. Religious hostility is rampant among the completely orthodox clergy, but is relatively uncommon among even the slightly less than orthodox. Yet it must be remembered that high orthodoxy with its resultant—religious hostility—is the modal clergy position.

Some insight into the mechanism by which absolute orthodoxy is transformed into religious hostility is provided by the fact that religious hostility is powerfully affected by particularism, which in turn is powerfully affected by orthodoxy (Table 15). Thus, while 88 per cent of those who felt belief in Jesus "probably has no influence" on salvation scored zero on religious hostility, only 29 per cent of those who responded that belief in Jesus was "absolutely necessary" for salvation scored zero.

Table 14.   ORTHODOXY AND RELIGIOUS HOSTILITY

	Orthodoxy Index				
	Low				High
	0	1	2	3	4
Number	(192)	(246)	(203)	(287)	(526)
Religious Hostility Index:					
Zero	75%	65%	55%	50%	16%
Low	23	32	35	40	26
Medium	2	3	8	7	29
High	0	0	2	3	29
	100%	100%	100%	100%	100%

Table 15 shows that particularism is the major mechanism linking orthodoxy with religious hostility. At all degrees of orthodoxy, particularism increases the probability of religious hostility. But among the zero orthodox, even among those who said one must believe in Jesus to be saved, more than two-thirds scored zero on religious hostility toward contemporary Jews. On the other hand, among the most orthodox (those who scored 4 on the index), 69 per cent of those who did not believe that one must accept Christ to be saved scored zero on religious hostility, while a mere handful (14 per cent) who took the completely particularistic position did so. These findings show that if orthodoxy is not accompanied by particularism, it need not, and often does not, lead to invidious religious conceptions of Jews, or (probably) of other non-Christians, either. Conversely, even among the unorthodox believers there is a tendency toward religious hostility if particularism is accepted. This finding is of both analytic and action importance. For it shows that if one could eradicate particularism, orthodoxy in and of itself would not normally lead to religious antagonism toward Jews. But as a practical matter, it must be recognized that to be an orthodox believer without also being a particularistic believer is extraordinarily rare: only 14 (or less than 3 per cent) of 526 clergymen (almost a third of the total) who scored high on orthodoxy rejected the absolute necessity of belief in Jesus for salvation. Thus, the largest single group of the Protestant clergy are orthodox, particularistic, and religiously hostile toward contemporary Jews.

Table 15.   ORTHODOXY, PARTICULARISM, AND RELIGIOUS HOSTILITY
(Per cent Zero on Religious Hostility Index)

	Orthodoxy Index				
	Low 0	1	2	3	High 4
Belief in Jesus vis-à-vis Salvation:					
"Probably has no influence"	82	100	86	100	—
Number	(28)	(13)	(7)[a]	(6)[a]	(1)
"Would probably help"	78	73	68	66	69
Number	(107)	(116)	(79)	(56)	(13)
"Absolutely necessary"	68	50	44	44	14
Number	(44)	(111)	(116)	(218)	(511)

[a] Too few cases for stable percentages; presented for descriptive interest only.

This takes us back to the starting point of this chapter. We saw there that about a third of all clergymen accept the historic guilt of Jews for the Crucifixion. At that time we indicated that this was in itself simply a facilitating factor: that if Christians did not extend this indictment to contemporary Jews it would be a matter of little importance. But, as we have seen, a substantial proportion of the clergy do connect the ancient and modern. Subsequent analysis showed that it is primarily the highly orthodox and highly particularistic clergy for whom blaming the Jews of Gospel times for the Crucifixion has implications for their current views of the religious condition of Jews. Clergymen at all levels of orthodoxy and particularism blame the ancient Jews for the Crucifixion. But our data showed that such belief has little effect on religious hostility among those low on orthodoxy and particularism. It is only among the more orthodox and more particularistic that the Crucifixion story implicating the Jews is appreciably related to hostility toward the modern Jews. Thus, the more modernist clergy who do blame the Crucifixion on the Jews seem to regard this as "ancient history." But for the more traditionally minded clergy these ancient crimes still live. To them the Crucifixion and the Jews' rejection of Jesus seem as recent as yesterday. Here are several explanations written in the margins of the questionnaire by clergymen:

A Missouri Synod Lutheran pastor wrote that he feels "sorry for all Jews who have rejected Jesus and thus have no God. There is only one God (Father-Son-Holy Ghost). 'He that knoweth not the Son honoreth not the Father,' said Jesus. The unrepentant Jew is unsaved. God loves the Jews and chose them, and my Saviour is a Jew. But they have chosen to reject Him. What more could they have wanted from the Messiah?"

A Southern Baptist: "The Jews were God's chosen people, although the Jew is out of fellowship with God. God is now dealing with the Jews and is preparing to bring them back to Him." [This pastor strongly agreed that "Jews have so much trouble because God is punishing them for rejecting Jesus." Perhaps this is partly what he meant in saying God is "dealing" with the Jews.]

A Missouri Synod Lutheran: "I don't have feelings one way or the other for a Jewish (nationality) person. I do have feelings and theological views which tell me that the Jew who hangs onto the Jewish faith is misled."

The Gospel accusations against the Jews for perpetrating the Crucifixion find fertile ground primarily among those who regard the Jews as automatically damned by virtue of rejecting Christianity. To the traditionally minded clergyman (as with his layman counterpart) it is not simply that nearly two thousand years ago a group of Jews were responsible for the death of Christ, but it was the ancestors of today's "damned" Jews who did it. And even if these conservative Christians should become convinced that the Jews are not suffering under the guilt of the Crucifixion they would still see the Jews as religious outcasts unless they converted.

In Table 16 all the pieces we have examined thus far are assembled. Our analysis has shown that orthodoxy and particularism both play a cumulative and independent role in generating religious hostility. Belief in the historic guilt of the Jews also contributes to religious hostility when combined with particularism and orthodoxy. Thus all three factors were included in a single measure which encompasses those key aspects of Christian teaching to which we attribute responsibility for tendencies to see contemporary Jews in a hostile religious light. We have identified this composite measure as the Doctrinal Index in an effort to find a descriptive label without pejorative connotations.[5] The index, in our judgment, taps basic Christian teachings none of which *necessarily* implies invidious judgments of Jews. The fact that such beliefs, as is shown in the table, are strongly related to holding a hostile religious image of the contemporary Jew is thus neither self-evident nor tautological, but rather reflects that set of linkages we have outlined previously.

Table 16.   DOCTRINAL INDEX AND RELIGIOUS HOSTILITY

	Doctrinal Index					
	Low 0	1	2	3	4	High 5
Per cent who scored zero on Religious Hostility Index	82	81	70	46	16	11
Number	(28)	(133)	(296)	(458)	(316)	(195)
Measures of Association:			Gamma		.691	
			Somers' DXY		.488	
Correlation Statistics:			Pearsonian *r*		.592	
			Kendall's Q		.806	

As the table shows, the relationship between these central elements of historic Christian doctrine and religious hostility toward the modern Jew is very large: while eight out of 10 scoring zero on the index also scored zero on religious hostility, only about one in ten of those scoring 5 on the index scored zero on religious hostility. This is very close to an "everyone and no one" finding and is almost identical in magnitude to the same relationship found among Protestant laymen. Thus, whether clergyman or layman, commitment to these doctrinal positions makes one highly susceptible to holding an invidious view of the religious status of Jews.

Religious Hostility Reappraised

At the beginning of this chapter we promised to reassess, in light of these new data based on the clergy, the thesis of *Christian Beliefs and Anti-Semitism* that orthodoxy leads through particularism through belief in historic Jewish guilt to a hostile religious conception of modern Jewry. What we have found is that the data for the clergy and the laity are almost identical. The clergy are about as likely as the laity to retain commitment to historic orthodoxy, to require belief in Jesus in order to be saved, and to blame the Jews both historically and down through the generations to modern times for the death of Jesus. Furthermore, the relationships among these factors are virtually identical for laymen and the clergy. The model provides as good a fit for the data based on the clergy as for those based on the laity.

By carrying the investigation to the clergy, we have provided an opportunity for the earlier findings to be falsified or at least greatly qualified by new evidence. But this simply did not occur. On the contrary, a number of counterinterpretations of the original findings do seem to be falsified or at least gravely threatened by this new evidence.

It is not possible to dismiss the process leading from orthodoxy to religious hostility toward modern Jews as a heterodox, nonchurch-related, religious aberration if the same process is found to occur with equal probability among the clergy. Not everything that happens to flocks can be blamed on the shepherds; but when both sheep and shepherds are wayward in the same direction and to the same degree, it seems unrealistic to blame only the sheep.

We still lack direct evidence that the clergy foster invidious religious images of the Jews among the laity. But presumably they would be as willing to relate their convictions to their members as they are to tell them to social scientists.

One final consideration will conclude this chapter. The earlier study emphasized the role of a hostile religious definition of Jews in predisposing Christians to accept nonreligious, anti-Semitic beliefs. In so doing it inadvertently deemphasized the explicit hostility of these religious conceptions as such, and it is now desirable to make amends for this oversight. While we are still concerned about the linkage between secular anti-Semitism and religious hostility and will devote the next chapter to assessing it, we must emphasize our concern about religious hostility in its own right. While purely secular and solely religious antagonism toward Jews can rightfully be regarded as analytically distinct, both are antagonistic. The fact that a Christian who believes God condones punishment of Jews, and that Jews remain guilty of the Crucifixion and are beyond redemption unless they convert, does not also believe that Jews cheat and connive, hardly means he harbors no anti-Jewish sentiments. It simply means that his hatred of Jews remains wholly religious. To a Jew, if not to those seeking the sources of anti-Semitism, it probably doesn't matter much whether a man hates you on religious grounds, secular grounds, or both. Hate is hate. And the religious images of the modern Jew which we have examined in this chapter are explicitly hateful.

4

Secular Anti-Semitism

So far we have found no appreciable differences between the clergy and the laity: they are about equally likely to accept traditional Christian doctrines about God, Jesus, the Devil, life beyond death, salvation, and the religious condition of the Jews. Thus far the model of the religious roots of anti-Semitism fits both groups equally well. But many clergymen, especially conservative ones, with whom the authors talked during conferences on the original findings felt that similarities between the clergy and the laity should end at this point. Many said that although they personally accepted the teaching that Jews are damned so long as they fail to convert, they did not believe this influenced their own general feelings about Jews. Some of these clergymen did acknowledge that there seemed to be some potential for ill will in conceptions of Jews as damned, but they steadfastly maintained that such beliefs produced no prejudice among them. They argued that Christian doctrines of love, brotherhood, compassion, and forgiveness simply flooded out any potential for prejudice contained in their Christian convictions.

In response to such statements, the authors granted the possibility that the clergy may well be able to suspend the potential for prejudice in their religious doctrines, but emphasized that the data showed that the laity often could not. Thus, the problem remained unchanged: so long as the religious model remained intact, the churches—whether intentionally or inadvertently—would be responsible for a good deal of anti-Semitism.

Yet, this exchange was so commonly a part of such conferences that considerable thought was given to the claim by conservative clergy that though the religious factors outlined by the authors did apply to them, they nonetheless were not led into anti-Semitism. Some of these claims could be dismissed because it was obvious the claimant simply couldn't recognize his own rather extensive prejudice toward Jews. But others seemed absolutely genuine. It appeared plausible that the clergy can compartmentalize the invidious implications of these doctrines for Jews and rely on the loving aspect of Christian teaching to sustain their beliefs, feelings, and actions toward Jews. After all, the clergy purport to be a major factor in promoting brotherhood and good will and are much more likely than are the laity to come into contact with persons of other faiths in situations which foster mutual respect and cooperation. Furthermore, it seemed plausible that the clergy, by token of their professional training and selection, would more often be committed to *both* Christian doctrine and Christian love; the latter has been found to be largely missing from lay religious commitment.[1] But although such possibilities were taken into serious consideration, the authors remained unconvinced that this could be the whole story. Even assuming that the clergy have a greater resistance to translating their religious potential for hostility against Jews into full-blown secular anti-Semitism, it is difficult to accept that this ability on the part of the clergy could wholly overcome this tendency. These thoughts can best be expressed by use of an analogy. Consider a line of men, some of them laymen, some clergy, running a foot race down a wharf. All run as fast as they can until they reach the edge of the wharf; then they try to stop. While agreeing that the clergy— since they have much more practice in the art of stopping themselves— would be less likely than the laity to fall off into the water, it would still be expected that some of the clergy would stumble in. (And, of course, laymen and clergy who don't run down the wharf at all get wet only by other methods.) The analogy seems apt because all persons who accept the explicitly hostile items examined in the preceding chapter are in the race and would have to stop themselves from accepting the many hostile secular images of Jews which are available in our culture.

We now examine the final link in our chain: secular anti-Semitism, that is, anti-Semitic beliefs and stereotypes which are not of a religious nature. Our premise is that persons whose religious outlook toward Jews is negative will be prone to accept negative secular definitions of Jews as well. In effect, we argue that it is relatively easy to regard Jews as untrustworthy, conniving, disloyal, and the like if one already believes them to be damned.

To test this assertion, it is necessary first to find means to establish how anti-Semitic the clergy are. To do so we have relied on two procedures: the first is the same as was used in the study of laymen; the second was tried for the first time with clergymen.

In the laymen study, respondents were presented with twenty-four statements about Jews and asked both to assess the truth of each and to decide whether each, supposing it were true, would cause them to feel hostile or friendly toward Jews. From these statements we selected the five which the largest proportion of respondents had indicated that, if true, would cause them to feel hostile toward Jews. These five were included in the clergy questionnaire. For each of these five statements the clergy were asked: "Would you decide whether you think Jews are like this or not?" The response categories were "Yes," "Somewhat," and "No." (The five items appear in Table 17.)[2]

In addition to repeating the main questions designed to measure anti-Semitism in the original study, we also decided to experiment with an item which takes attitudes toward Jews head on. Immediately following the specific questions about Jews we asked the following self-appraisal:

> All in all, as you assess your feelings about Jews, which of the following statements comes closest to representing the way you feel about them? (Please check only one.)
> 1. Frankly, looking inside myself, I tend to feel somewhat hostile toward Jews.
> 2. There are many individual Jews whom I admire but I feel that I do harbor some ill feelings toward Jews in a general way.
> 3. I believe I can honestly say that I have no ill feelings about Jews at all though I am not disposed to favor them over other groups.
> 4. Not only do I bear no resentment toward Jews, but I feel particularly drawn to them in a positive way.
> 5. None of the above comes close to representing my feelings. I feel _____.

Having never pretested this item, we were not at all sure how useful it would prove to be. It might simply show that people, even clergymen, are blind to their own prejudices or at least can only admit them piecemeal, not making a general admission of ill will. On the other hand, it seemed worth trying, particularly with a group such as clergymen who might feel a special obligation to examine their feelings and to make them known.

There are several reasons to suppose that the clergy will be somewhat less prone to anti-Semitism than are laymen. For one thing, the clergy have a higher average education than do church members, and we know from other studies that there is a fairly strong negative correlation between education and anti-Semitism.[3] Second, in recent years clergymen have been repeatedly exposed to various programs to eradicate prejudice and increase brotherhood on the assumption that the clergy can play a major role in influencing their parishioners on such matters. Presumably this exposure has not been wholly fruitless. And finally, the clergy may be more competent than laymen at encapsulating the religious basis for hostility toward Jews, thereby severing the connection between religious hostility and secular anti-Semitism.

As it turned out in our data, the clergy are less likely than were laymen in the earlier study to hold anti-Semitic beliefs. Table 17 shows the proportion of clergy answering "yes" that Jews are like this or "somewhat" like this for each of the five items. Totals for laymen are shown at the extreme right.

It will be seen that 10 per cent of the clergy believe that "Jews are more likely than Christians to cheat in business," although within denominational groupings the range of agreement varies from 6 per cent of the Methodists and Episcopalians, through 15 per cent of American Baptists and Missouri Lutherans, to 19 per cent of Southern Baptists. By way of comparison, 33 per cent of Protestant laymen accepted this same item, or about three times the proportion among the clergy. Denominational differences, however, were much the same, with Methodists and Episcopalians being much less likely to endorse the item than were Southern Baptists.

Returning to the clergy, the second item in Table 17—"Because Jews are not bound by Christian ethics, they will do things to get ahead that Christians generally will not do"—elicited greater agreement: 20 per cent over all. The biggest shifts came among clergy of the more con-

Table 17. CLERGY IMAGES OF THE JEW BY DENOMINATION

	United Church of Christ	Metho-dist	Epis-copal	Presby-terian	Luth. Church in Amer.	Amer. Luth. Church	American Baptist	Mis-souri Lutheran	South. Baptist	Total Prot. Clergy	Total Prot. Laity
Number	(137)	(354)	(207)	(226)	(87)	(118)	(147)	(134)	(170)	(1,580)	
"Jews are more likely than Christians to cheat in business."											
Per cent "Yes" and "Somewhat"	12[a]	6	6	9	9	12	15	15	19	10	33
"Because Jews are not bound by Christian ethics, they do things to get ahead that Christians generally will not do."											
Per cent "Yes" and "Somewhat"	18	13	11	17	17	15	28	31	41	20	36
"Jews want to remain different from other people, and yet they are touchy if people notice these differences."											
Per cent "Yes" and "Somewhat"	61	46	48	48	55	59	57	49	53	51	57
"Jews, in general, are inclined to be more loyal to Israel than to America."											
Per cent "Yes" and "Somewhat"	17	14	14	16	21	23	27	24	31	19	31
"Jews are less likely than Christians to oppose Communism."											
Per cent "Yes" and "Somewhat"	18	7	15	10	15	13	17	20	18	13	15

[a] Percentages in each case based only on those clergy who answered the question.

servative denominations: 28 per cent of the American Baptists, 31 per cent of the Missouri Lutherans, and 41 per cent of the Southern Baptists agreed that Jews will do unethical things to get ahead. On this item the clergy more closely approximated the responses of the laity, 36 per cent of whom answered "yes" or "somewhat" to this same item.

On the third item in the table—"Jews want to remain different from other people, and yet they are touchy if people notice these differences" —half of the clergy agreed, only a little less than found among laymen, 57 per cent of whom agreed. By denomination, 46 per cent of the Methodist clergy agreed, while 59 per cent of the American Lutherans and 61 per cent of United Church of Christ clergy did so.

The fourth and fifth items in the table raise the question of Jewish patriotism. The fourth item—"Jews, in general, are inclined to be more loyal to Israel than to America"—shows that about one of five clergymen (19 per cent) accepted this belief about Jews, whereas about three in ten (31 per cent) of Protestant laymen gave this response. Among both laity and clergy there are considerable denominational differences: while 14 per cent of the Methodist and Episcopalian clergy suspected Jews of greater loyalty to Israel than to America, 27 per cent of the American Baptists and 31 per cent of the Southern Baptists did so.

The final item in the table finds the clergy and the laity equally willing to believe that "Jews are less likely than Christians to oppose Communism." This belief is not widespread in either group (13 per cent of the clergy and 15 per cent of the laity), but again denomination makes a difference, with the Methodists being the least and the Missouri Lutherans and Southern Baptists most prone to accept this item.

There are several ways of evaluating these findings. On the one hand, there are grounds for optimism. On each of the four most invidious statements about Jews the vast majority of the clergy—80 per cent or more—said "no." We suspect that these findings are considerably different from what would have been found had a similar study been done of the clergy even ten or fifteen years ago. There has probably been a good deal of improvement in clergy attitudes toward Jews, and the over-all picture today looks rather good. On the other hand, considering the fact that the church is *the* institution traditionally concerned with representing man's highest ideals, and juxtaposing the evidence that among the ordained servants of this institution one in ten thinks Jews cheat in business and two in ten think Jews will act unethically to get ahead and are more loyal to a foreign power than to America, there seem no grounds for complacency. Although the clergy are much less infected with anti-Semitism than they might be and probably much less so than they used to be, when we examine responses to these five items in combination and see that only 37 per cent of the clergy rejected all of them as untrue, we must also recognize that the clergy are a good deal more anti-Semitic than they ought to be.

How do ministers' responses to these statements about Jews correspond with their assessments of their own feelings toward Jews? To answer this question as well as to facilitate our subsequent analysis, it is necessary to have a more reliable measure of anti-Semitic belief than can be provided by the items taken individually. Thus an Anti-Semitism Index was constructed (Table 18). It may be helpful to think of this index as a quiz made up of five questions in which "yes" is the wrong answer to each, "somewhat" is at least partly wrong, and "no" is correct. Consequently, for each "yes" answer a respondent was given 2 points, for each "somewhat" 1 point, and zero points for each "no." In this quiz, those with the most points fail. (Only those who answered all five items were included in the scoring.) In raw form, the index scores ranged from 10 (for answering "yes" to all five) to zero (for answering "no" on all five), and the index is skewed toward the bottom. While 37 per cent of the clergy scored zero (the perfect A students, to pursue the quiz analogy), only seven clergymen scored 10 (total failures). In this extended, raw form the index is much too unwieldy to use; thus it had to be collapsed— the equivalent of assigning letter grades to various ranges of numerical quiz scores. Even if we used the index uncollapsed, the problem of assigning some meaning to various ranges of scores would still have to be faced. We know what zero and 10 mean, but what about those who scored in between? Whom shall we call anti-Semitic?

Table 18.   CLERGY SCORES ON THE ANTI-SEMITISM INDEX

	37%	None
	46	Low
	17	Medium to High
	100%	
Number	(1,431)[a]	

[a] Index built only for those respondents who answered all five items.

Our solution was to retain the purity of the zero scorers and identify them as "None" on the Anti-Semitism Index. Those who scored 1 or 2 were combined to provide the Low category. Persons in this category did not exceed responding either "somewhat" on two of the five items or "yes" on one of them. Now, obviously, this does not indicate much anti-Semitic belief, which is why that group was labeled Low, but to fall into this category is quite different from exhibiting no anti-Semitism. Finally, all who scored from 3 to 10 points on the index were classified in a third category labeled Medium to High.

Table 18 shows the distribution of the clergy scores on the Anti-Semitism Index. Thirty-seven per cent scored none, an additional 46 per cent scored Low, and 17 per cent scored Medium to High. By way of contrast, 20 per cent of the laity scored None on anti-Semitism. This again confirms our findings on the individual items, with the clergy showing more resistance to anti-Semitism than do the laity: one of five laymen rejected all these anti-Semitic statements, while nearly two of five clergy did so. On the other hand, among both clergy and laity, the great majority accepted the accuracy of some of these negative items about Jews, although few in either group exhibited really rabid anti-Semitism by accepting them all.

In the study of laymen a good deal of attention was devoted to establishing the validity of this index as a measure of anti-Semitism, and it is not necessary to repeat that discussion here. Suffice it to say that the items have face validity—both in our judgment and in that of our respondents these beliefs would provide a legitimate basis for ill will toward Jews if they were true—and the index proved to be an accurate predictor of responses to other anti-Semitic statements not included in it.

By including the opportunity for individual clergymen to assess the general tone of their own feelings toward Jews in the present study, we have an additional resource for assessing the validity of the index. As mentioned earlier, we inserted this question without knowing whether it would prove at all workable. That is, would it draw out differences among the clergy or would everyone simply take the neutral response category?[4] As it turned out, the item was neither wholly successful nor a complete failure. There was a distinct tendency for the respondents to pile up in the neutral category (64 per cent did so), and a very few clergymen (only ten) admitted open hostility toward Jews. However, a small minority (7 per cent) did say they harbored some "ill feelings toward Jews," and a larger minority (18 per cent) claimed to feel particularly positive toward Jews. This offers an estimate of considerably less anti-Semitism among the clergy than is indicated by the index based on their beliefs about Jews.

Table 19.   SUBJECTIVE ASSESSMENTS OF FEELINGS TOWARD JEWS AND THE ANTI-SEMITISM INDEX

	Feels "somewhat hostile"	Has "some ill feelings"	Neutral	Has "positive" feelings
Anti-Semitism Score:				
Zero	11%	18%	37%	48%
Low	44	52	46	41
Medium–High	44	30	17	11
Per cent	99a	100	100	100
Number	(9)	(99)	(944)	(256)

aColumn fails to add to 100 because of rounding error.

Nevertheless, the findings based on the self-assessments of the clergy shown in Table 19 provide some confirmation of the validity of the Anti-Semitism Index. The proportions scoring zero on the Anti-Semitism Index systematically increase from 11 to 48 per cent as personal assessments move from the negative to the positive. Similarly, the proportions scored Medium to High on the index decline across the same spectrum: from 44 to 11 per cent. But it must also be recognized that while these patterns offer confirmation of the index, the correlation between objective and subjective measures is far from perfect. Some who admit to prejudice were scored as unprejudiced on the index, and a much larger number who admit no prejudice or who even claim to have positive feelings about Jews were scored as prejudiced on the index. Which classification is correct: the one earned by answering our belief items or the one claimed through self-assessment? To answer this question we made more intensive examination of the deviant cases. The findings seem most profitable for understanding the nature of prejudice.

It is no surprise that some portion of clergymen could be unwitting or self-deceived about their own prejudice: that they can both agree to the truth of anti-Semitic statements and deny they are anti-Semitic.[5] Denials of having any personal dislike of "nigras" by Southern Klansmen are all too familiar, as are remarks that begin, "Now, I've got nothing against Hebes, you understand. . . ." Thus, some lack of correspondence between objective and subjective measures of anti-Semitism is to be expected. In order to demonstrate that this interpretation is correct and establish that the objective is the better measure, further exploration of this group's outlook is required.

Yet what are we to make of the other kind of deviant case: clergymen who confessed negative feelings toward Jews, but nevertheless scored zero on the Anti-Semitism Index? One possibility is that we simply failed to include items which tapped their particular basis for antipathy toward Jews. But a second explanation seemed to us more likely. As one of the authors remarked when shown the computer output reported in Table 18, "Those are the overconscientious liberals." What he meant was that some clergymen who are especially concerned about prejudice are inclined to fear that because they grew up in a prejudiced society they may still bear some yet undiscovered taint of prejudice. If data can be found which show that these deviant cases are, in fact, strongly committed to fighting prejudice, this, too, would prompt greater confidence in the objective as opposed to the subjective measure.

Our initial attempts to unravel these questions gave confidence to our interpretations. A number of ministers wrote comments in the margins of the questionnaire intended to explain responses to particular questions. Examining some of those written by ministers of one or the other deviant types yielded the following insights.

Ministers we would classify as self-deceived about their own prejudice (scored as anti-Semitic but who claimed neutral or positive feelings) wrote the following:

Case 1: "Yes, they are more likely to cheat than are *real* Christians. . . . [He qualified his claim to feel especially positive toward Jews this way]: I feel I should tell them of Jesus, whom they rejected 1968 years ago."

Case 2: "I have deep compassion for Jews—they need my Messiah."

Case 3: "I have concern for these people because they deny Jesus to be the Son of God. I believe that any person who does this is eternally lost. . . . Not all people of Jewish race deny Jesus."

Case 4: "I generally admire the religious fervor of Hebrew Christians [thus limiting the kind of Jews toward whom he claims to feel particularly positive]. I resent the separatism and aggressiveness of many Jews when I compare them with people of other cultures."

Case 5: "I try to take men one at a time as they are. Percentages of Jews tending to *push* (respondent's emphasis) seem to run higher than among . . . Christians, but I would not want to generalize here."

Ministers we suspect of overconscientiousness wrote the following qualifications of their admissions of harboring some ill will toward Jews:

Case 6: "I probably have been touched by anti-Semitic feelings from childhood; but I am pro-Israel and after seeing the horror of genocide in WWII, I have enormous sympathy for the Jewish people."

Case 7: "I bear a mixed feeling of intellectually, religiously, and friendship-wise acquired positive attitudes; but carry with me from youth culturally acquired anti-Semitism."

Case 8: "For no other reason than strangeness and cultural differences. By association these can be overcome; feelings are emotional, nonrational."

Case 9: "I'm somewhat between No. 2 and No. 3. I do not 'harbor' ill feelings; I deal with them and overcome them. Prejudice I have—but prejudice I do not want for I know many Jews and want to love them as any other people."

These cues from written comments are, of course, hardly conclusive. Since most clergymen wrote nothing on this page, remarks such as those above provide no systematic evidence that the deviant types are predominantly as we believe them to be. However, some more rigorous testing of our notions was possible. Cross-classifying objective and subjective measures of anti-Semitism produces nine types,[6] as is shown in Figure 2. We have inserted a brief characterization of each type according to the hypotheses developed above. For ease of reference we have also assigned each a number. Thus, Type 1 we have identified as the overconscientious: persons who confessed prejudice, but exhibited none on the objective measure. Types 6 and 9 are the other main deviant cells in the typology; we have characterized them as the self-deceived anti-Semites and the extremely self-deceived anti-Semites, respectively. The former claim neutral feelings toward Jews, but scored Medium to High on the objective index. The latter claim particularly positive feelings toward Jews, but also scored Medium to High on the Anti-Semitism Index.

Figure 2. A TYPOLOGY OF OBJECTIVE AND SUBJECTIVE ANTI-SEMITISM

Subjective Assessment of Feelings toward Jews:

Objective:	Admits Ill Feelings [a]	Claims Neutral Feelings	Claims Positive Feelings
Score on Anti-Semitism Index Zero	TYPE 1 THE OVER-CONSCIENTIOUS N = 19 % = 1	TYPE 4 THE UNBIASED N = 345 % = 26	TYPE 7 THE PRO-SEMITES N = 123 % = 9
Low	TYPE 2 THE MODERATELY PREJUDICED SELF-AWARES N = 55 % = 4	TYPE 5 THE MODERATELY PREJUDICED SELF-DECEIVED N = 436 % = 33	TYPE 8 THE MODERATELY PREJUDICED QUITE SELF-DECEIVED N = 105 % = 8
Medium to High	TYPE 3 THE CONSCIOUS ANTI-SEMITES N = 34 % = 3	TYPE 6 THE SELF-DECEIVED ANTI-SEMITES N = 163 % = 12	TYPE 9 THE EXTREMELY SELF-DECEIVED ANTI-SEMITES N = 28 % = 2 [b]

[a] Categories 1 and 2 on item collapsed.
[b] Percentages fail to add to 100 because of rounding error.

To test the accuracy of this classification of the deviant cases, its adequacy to support our case, we examined their beliefs and actions on other relevant questions. The findings ought to show that clergymen of Type 1 most closely resemble Types 4 and 7, those who showed no bias on the objective measure and characterized themselves as neutral or particularly positive toward Jews. Similarly, we hypothesize that the self-deceived (Types 6 and 9) will most resemble the conscious anti-Semites of Type 3.

This is precisely what the data show. Theologically, the ministers of Type 1 were almost identical with those of Type 7: these two types were overwhelmingly the most modernist clergy among the types (as measured on the Doctrinalism Index). Conversely Types 6 and 9 (the self-deceived) were overwhelmingly the most theologically traditional among the types and most closely matched the conscious anti-Semites of Type 3.

Similar patterns occurred on civil rights activism. The overconscientious clergy of Type 1 tended to be activists on behalf of racial justice, most closely resembling the clergy of Type 7 whom we classify as pro-Semitic. Half of the Type 1 clergy had attended a protest meeting on civil rights (two-thirds of the Type 7's had done so) and a third had participated in a civil rights march (44 per cent of the Type 7's). The self-deceived (Types 6 and 9) were overwhelmingly inactive on civil rights and were virtually indistinguishable in this regard from the conscious anti-Semites of Type 3: 11 per cent of the 6's and 9's and 10 per cent of the 3's had participated in a civil rights march. Furthermore, on all these comparisons the objective measure of anti-Semitism was a much better predictor of civil rights activism than was the subjective measure.

These findings, we believe, amply demonstrate that the deviant cases are predominantly as we suspected, the overconscientious on the one hand and self-deceiving on the other. This lends considerable confidence to the validity of the Anti-Semitism Index. But it also introduces a further note of pessimism about our findings. For the fact is that overconscientiousness is rather rare among the clergy, while self-deception is rather common. Indeed, the self-deceived are ten times more numerous than the overconscientious (191/19), and among those clergymen who scored Medium to High on the Anti-Semitism Index an overwhelming 85 per cent failed to recognize, or at least to admit, that they harbor any ill will toward Jews! Such persons constitute 14 per cent of the entire sample. If the moderately prejudiced self-deceived (Types 5 and 8) are also included, 55 per cent of the clergy qualify. Anti-Semitism may not be rampant among the clergy, but neither is self-awareness.

We turn now to the major question of this study: Do the religious sources of anti-Semitism which influenced the attitudes and feelings of the laity toward Jews also operate among the clergy?

In answering this question we first examined the relationships between anti-Semitism (measured by the index), orthodoxy, particularism, and the belief that the historic Jews were responsible for the Crucifixion. We found that all three religious factors had a significant and mutually independent effect on secular anti-Semitism.

It will be recalled from Chapter 3 that these three religious components were combined into a single measure which we called the Doctrinal Index. Table 20 shows that the Doctrinal Index does, indeed, have a rather strong effect on anti-Semitism. The rejection of anti-Semitic statements by the clergy falls systematically from left to right across the table as their commitment to traditional Christian doctrines increases. Thus, of those clergy least committed to traditional doctrines (zero on the Doctrinal Index), 56 per cent rejected every anti-Semitic item, while only 7 per cent fell into the Medium to High category. But of those clergy most committed to traditional doctrines (5 on the Doctrinal Index), only 20 per cent resisted all five items. Indeed, more than twice as many of these clergymen (42 per cent) fell into the Medium to High category as scored None (20 per cent).

Table 20. DOCTRINALISM AND ANTI-SEMITISM

	Doctrinal Index					
	Low					High
	0	1	2	3	4	5
Number	(27)	(126)	(276)	(432)	(318)	(185)
Score on Index of Anti-Semitic Beliefs:						
None	56%	50%	46%	35%	32%	20%
Low	37	46	44	49	47	39
Medium to High	7	4	9	16	21	42
	100%	100%	99%ᵃ	100%	100%	101%ᵃ

ᵃColumn fails to add to 100 because of rounding error.

Although *the clergy are less likely than the laity to be anti-Semitic,* these findings show that for those clergy who are, *their anti-Semitism is more powerfully related to religious convictions* than is true of laymen. Among laymen, although these same doctrinal factors were related to anti-Semitism, only an 18 percentage-point difference obtained on the proportions scored None on anti-Semitism between the highest and lowest points on doctrinalism. Table 19 shows twice as great a per- centage-point difference (35 points) among the clergy. *To this extent the explanatory model is a better fit for the clergy than for the laity.* This difference is easily understood. Research has shown that greater cogni- tive consistency is to be found among those whose role or training tends to make manifest contradictory beliefs. The religious views of the clergy ought, on the average, to be more mutually consistent than those of the laity. Thus, if there is a compatibility between certain religious doctrines and anti-Semitism, the clergy should be more likely than the laity to recognize and accept these conclusions. Again we must emphasize the greater resistance of the clergy to anti-Semitism. Nevertheless, the data show that, among the clergy, anti-Semitism is more highly correlated with their religious convictions than was the case among church-members.

The Doctrinal Index is, of course, only one link in the chain of religious factors which we believe leads to anti-Semitism. Indeed, in the study of laymen it was found that doctrinalism had no independent role in fostering secular anti-Semitism. Rather these doctrines led to anti-Semitism because they first led to a hostile religious definition of the modern Jew, and it was this which in turn led to secular anti-Semitism. Put another way, the link between doctrinalism and anti-Semitism was found to be wholly religious hostility: only through religious hostility did doctrinalism lead to anti-Semitism.

In the last chapter we saw that there was a strong relationship between doctrinalism and religious hostility toward Jews. Clergy who scored high on the Doctrinal Index were very unlikely to exhibit no religious hostility (only 11 per cent did not), while those who scored low on doctrinalism were extremely likely to be without a trace of religious hostility (81 per cent were). The correlation coefficients between the two indices ranged from .49 to .81, depending on the statistical measure used.[7] Thus, this part of the linkage holds. We have also just seen that doctrinalism is positively related to anti-Semitism. We must now see the extent to which religious hostility is, in fact, the linking mechanism between the two. If religious hostility is the main reason why the doctrinalism-anti-Semitism relationship occurs, the relationship between the two ought to disappear when religious hostility is statistically controlled.[8]

In Table 21 this interpretation is assessed. It can readily be seen that the findings here are not precisely like those found for the laity. Religious hostility has a potent effect on anti-Semitism, but it does not entirely account for the relationship between doctrinalism and anti-Semitism. Instead, the interconnections of these variables are more complex among clergymen than among the laity.

As among laymen, where religious hostility is lacking, doctrinalism has virtually no effect on anti-Semitism. Looking across the first row of the table—only ministers who scored zero on religious hostility—the

Table 21. DOCTRINALISM, RELIGIOUS HOSTILITY, AND ANTI-SEMITISM

(Per cent of respondents who ranked Medium–High on Index of Anti-Semitism)

	Doctrinal Index						Correlation Coefficients			
	Low					High				
Rank on Index of Religious Hostility toward Jews	0	1	2	3	4	5	DXY	r	G	Q
0	9	3	5	13	14	14	.09	.13	.16	.16
Number	(22)	(103)	(191)	(193)	(42)	(21)				
1	—	5	13	16	14	25	.12	.16	.19	.17
Number	(5)	(21)	(77)	(191)	(86)	(36)				
2	—	—	—	29	22	42				
Number	(0)	(1)	(6)	(34)	(87)	(53)				
3	—	—	—	25[a]	31	63	.26	.20	.40	.57
Number	(0)	(0)	(2)	(8)	(64)	(67)				
Original relationship between Doctrinal Index and Medium–High anti-Semitism	7	4	9	16	21	42	.20	.27	.32	.31
Number	(27)	(126)	(276)	(432)	(318)	(185)				

[a] Too few cases for stable percentage; presented for descriptive interest only.

proportion who scored Medium to High on anti-Semitism rises only very slightly from left to right. The increase in anti-Semitism with doctrinalism is only slightly greater among those who scored 1 on religious hostility. But looking at clergy who scored a maximum of 3 on religious hostility, we see that doctrinalism retains a fairly strong independent effect; the proportions scoring Medium to High on anti-Semitism increase from 25 per cent to 31 per cent to 63 per cent, moving from 3 to 5 on doctrinalism. Looking down the columns of the table, a similar pattern can be seen: religious hostility mainly affects anti-Semitism among those highest on doctrinalism. As doctrinalism scores decrease, the impact of religious hostility also decreases; thus there is a 49 percentage-point difference in anti-Semitism between those highest and lowest on religious hostility among clergymen with maximum scores on doctrinalism. These differences, however, drop to 16 percentage points among those with scores of 4 on doctrinalism and to 12 percentage points among those who scored 3. Thus it is not simply that religious hostility is a necessary linkage between religious doctrine and anti-Semitism, as was true among the laity, but that religious hostility loses most of its force when not accompanied by unwavering commitment to traditional doctrines. Among laymen, religious hostility produced anti-Semitism even among those with only moderate or no commitment to traditional theology. Thus religious hostility wiped out all independent effects of doctrinalism. But among the clergy the anti-Semitic potential of religious hostility weakens markedly as soon as strict doctrinal commitment is absent. This is why doctrinalism seems to retain an independent effect among the clergy, while it did not among the laity. For the clergy, both doctrinalism and religious hostility tend to be necessary to produce anti-Semitism; when either is lacking, the transformation of religiousness into anti-Semitism is considerably curtailed. Yet it must also be recognized that the two do tend to occur together, and the ministers high on both are considerably more numerous than those lacking both.

While all these findings in Table 21 are important, the major finding is to be seen along the diagonal from the upper left to the lower right of the table. There the joint effect of doctrinalism and religious hostility can be seen; and it is a powerful effect, indeed. In the upper left of the table the proportions who scored Medium to High on anti-Semitism are uniformly low: 9 per cent, 3 per cent, 5 per cent. In the lower right-hand corner the proportions who are anti-Semitic are quite high: 31 per cent, 42 per cent, and 63 per cent. Indeed, there is a 54 percentage-point difference in anti-Semitism between those lowest and those highest on doctrinalism and religious hostility.

These findings provide solid confirmation of our case that Christian religious commitment contains a considerable potential for fostering anti-Semitism. Among both clergymen and laymen those most committed to traditional Christian teachings are much more likely than those who have adopted modernist theological views to exhibit anti-Semitism.

The role of religion in fostering anti-Semitism is even clearer in Table 22, which presents the data of Table 21 in a different form. Here we have created a compound dependent variable by combining the measures of religious hostility and anti-Semitism. This produced four types of respondents:

1. Those who exhibit both religious hostility and anti-Semitism (14 per cent).
2. Those with religious hostility, but without anti-Semitism (42 per cent).
3. Those who are anti-Semitic, but without religious hostility (4 per cent).
4. Those who are neither religiously hostile nor anti-Semitic (40 per cent).

The table shows how clergymen at different points on the Doctrinal Index are distributed among these types.

Over all, the clergy are remarkably free of anti-Semitism which is *not* rooted in religious hostility. Of the total, only 4 per cent exhibited anti-Semitism unaccompanied by religious hostility (the third row across the table). Furthermore, this variety of anti-Semitism is not related to doctrinalism, but is about equally common at all points across the scale. This makes more readily apparent what we concluded from inspection of Table 21: *traditional doctrines produce anti-Semitism primarily by first producing religious hostility.*

Furthermore, it is also easily seen in Table 22 that the linkage between religious hostility and anti-Semitism is not inevitable. Among clergymen low on doctrinalism this linkage virtually never occurs. It is true that these clergymen are much less inclined than are conservatives to

Table 22. DOCTRINALISM, RELIGIOUS HOSTILITY, AND ANTI-SEMITISM

Religiously Hostile[a] Number	Anti-Semitic[b]	Doctrinal Index						
		Low 0 (27)	1 (125)	2 (276)	3 (426)	4 (279)	High 5 (177)	Total (1,310)
1. Yes	Yes	0%	1%	6%	10%	18%	41%	14%
2. Yes	No	19	17	24	45	67	47	42
3. No	Yes	7	2	4	6	2	2	4
4. No	No	74	80	66	40	13	10	40
		100%	100%	100%	101%c	100%	100%	100%

Braces combining rows 1 and 2: Low 19, 1: 55, 2: 18, 3: 85, 4: 30, High 88.

[a] *Yes* includes all who expressed any religious hostility; *No*, those who scored zero on the index.
[b] *Yes* includes those Medium to High on the Index of Anti-Semitic Belief; *No*, Low and zero.
c Column fails to add up to 100 because of rounding error.

hold religiously hostile views in the first place. But those who do, prevent it from corrupting their secular beliefs about Jews. Thus while 19 per cent of those who scored zero on doctrinalism exhibited religious hostility, not one combined this with secular anti-Semitism. Among those who scored 1 only 1 per cent combined hostility and anti-Semitism, although 17 per cent were classified as religiously hostile. Among those who scored 2, only 6 per cent (of 30 per cent) connected religious hostility and anti-Semitism.

The ability of the clergy to compartmentalize their religious views about Jews begins to collapse as we examine the more doctrinally conservative clergy. Among those who scored 5 on doctrinalism, 88 per cent exhibited religious hostility, and nearly half of these (41 per cent) also scored Medium to High on the Anti-Semitism Index.

At the beginning of this chapter we admitted that there might be some truth to claims by conservative clergymen that they can believe in the eternal damnation of the Jews, but not permit this to spill over into anti-Semitism. Our data show that this claim is partly justified. Indeed, to return to our analogy about racing to the end of a wharf, the theologically liberal clergy seem to be almost uniformly competent at stopping short of the water's edge. Even among the most conservative, half are able to stop. But half also fall off into anti-Semitism. It is obvious in Table 22, therefore, as it was in the study of laymen, that the best way to keep dry is not to run in the religious hostility race at all.

This would seem to have important implications for church action. Had doctrinalism alone been the major factor in producing anti-Semitism, methods of curbing the latter would have been difficult to suggest, aside from awaiting further secularization of the faith. One could not really have asked conservative Christians to change their conceptions of God, Christ, the afterlife, or the requirements for eternal salvation. But the data show that this is unnecessary. The key factor is religious hostility: conceptions of contemporary Jews as unforgiven for the Crucifixion and under a curse from God. If these could be eliminated from the Christian consciousness, considerable progress toward disconnecting the transformation of Christian commitment into anti-Semitism would be made.

At first glance this would seem a feasible project for Christians to undertake, and it was the main thrust of the authors' suggestions to church leaders following the publication of the earlier study. After all, most Christian bodies had officially rejected or substantially qualified these hostile religious judgments of contemporary Jews. Thus the task was not to change doctrines, but to promulgate them. And this, too, seemed feasible, since it was the most faithful church members who most needed to be reeducated, and presumably these would be the easiest members for the churches to reach.

But in light of the present findings we realize such optimism was unjustified. For us as sociologists, it is embarrassing to admit that institutions were judged by their formal proclamations. It was naïve to assume so close a correspondence between the official position of the churches, as expressed by their leaders, and what was really true of the rank-and-file clergy of those same churches.

On the basis of official church teachings, hostile religious images of the Jews need not, and indeed should not, follow from commitment to traditional Christian doctrines. But as found earlier among the laity, and now among the clergy, too, in practice they nearly always do. Only 11 per cent of the clergy and 7 per cent of the laymen who scored highest on doctrinalism rejected the religious hostility items.

This suggests that there is a powerful cognitive compatibility between doctrinalism and religious hostility which cannot be banished by mere official fiat. Considerable educational effort will undoubtedly be required. Furthermore, before any such effort can be launched effectively it will be necessary for the churches to convince their own clergy of the official doctrines. Until this is done there are no means for reaching the laity. This is a more pessimistic situation than we imagined. From the earlier study the path seemed clear. But so long as the clergy are as unlikely as the laity to see it, we have been expecting the blind to lead the blind.

To complete the replication portion of this study, we now employ a technique called "path analysis" which has recently come into use among social scientists.[9] Path analysis is an adaptation of conventional multiple regression procedures. Its purpose is to test the fit between a sequential causal model and an appropriate body of quantitative data. Findings permit the construction of a path diagram—a depiction of the relationships among the chosen variables. Thus, while the underlying statistical techniques may prove baffling to nonspecialists, the findings are easier to grasp and to compare than are less statistically complex, but visually more confusing, percentage tables. Ease of comparison is especially important because we have used the path analysis technique not only on the clergy data but also to reassess the data on laymen. Thus a direct comparison of two simple path diagrams and a small number of normalized regression coefficients will clarify the extent to which we have successfully replicated the earlier study as well as permit a summary assessment of the fit of our model to each body of data.

Path analysis is perhaps most appropriate when it is subsequent to an extensive tabular analysis of the data. Its particular advantage lies in the fact that it permits simultaneous examination of a greater number of variables than is usually possible in a tabular analysis. In the tabular analysis presented in this study, and in the laymen study as well, it was necessary to merge various concepts and indices as we proceeded in order to carry the analysis forward without running out of cases. Thus, orthodoxy, particularism, and the image of the historic Jews were merged into the Doctrinal Index before secular anti-Semitism could be brought into the analysis. But path analysis permits examining the operation of the whole model without such merging.

Some critics of the laymen study argued that in merging various measures of religious beliefs in order to proceed with the tabular analysis we had perhaps contaminated our results. Specifically, it was argued that by including the historic image of the Jews as Crucifiers in a single index along with orthodoxy and particularism we had spuriously linked these factors to secular anti-Semitism when in fact only the historic image was so linked. We were not impressed with these arguments. It was apparent in the tabular analysis that such could not be the case. Nevertheless, we regretted not having included some form of regression analysis in that study in order to increase confidence in and understanding of our findings. We now rectify that omission.

Path Analysis: The Lay Sample

Path analysis provides a series of regression coefficients, one for each logically possible two-variable relationship. These coefficients indicate the extent to which each pair is related independently of other variables in the model and according to a specified time order among the variables. In keeping with our theoretical model as developed and analyzed earlier in the study, we specified the order of the variables as follows: (1)

Orthodoxy, (2) Particularism, (3) Historical Jews as Crucifiers, (4) Religious Hostility, (5) Secular Anti-Semitism. Thus, orthodoxy is the start of the causal sequence of the model and secular anti-Semitism is specified as the end product, or consequence. Using Alan Wilson's WLSQ program, normalized regression coefficients were computed for all possible pairs among these five variables. The test of the fit between our model and the data is relatively straightforward. The direct causal path specified by our model ought to show relatively large normalized regression coefficients. Paths disregarded by our theoretical model should yield relatively small or nonexistent normalized regression coefficients. That this is the case can easily be seen in Figure 3. In order to make the path diagram more graphically effective, the thickness of the arrows marking the various paths has been made proportional to the size of their normalized regression coefficients: the wider the arrow, the larger the coefficient.

The first obvious finding shown in the diagram is that virtually the only path from Christian beliefs to secular anti-Semitism is through religious hostility. The coefficient for the direct path from orthodoxy to anti-Semitism, for example, is a meaningless —.03, for the direct path from particularism to anti-Semitism it is only .09, and for the direct

Figure 3. PATH ANALYSIS (LAYMEN SAMPLE)

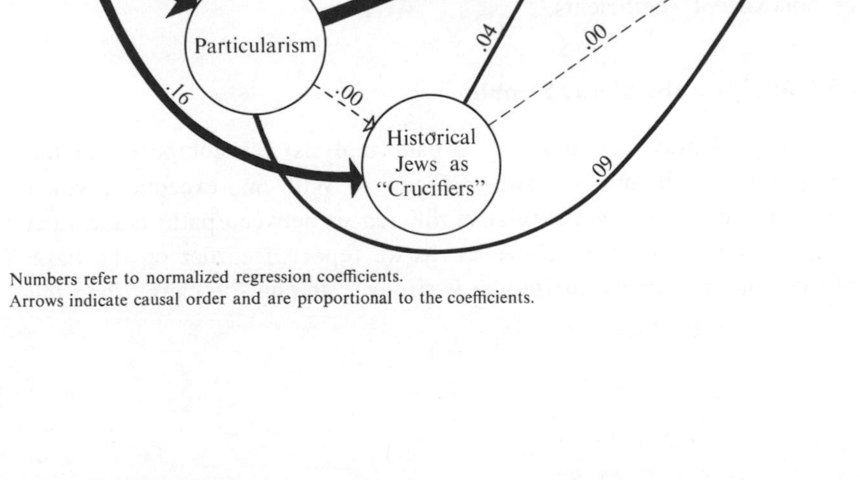

Numbers refer to normalized regression coefficients.
Arrows indicate causal order and are proportional to the coefficients.

path from the historical image of the Jews as Crucifiers to anti-Semitism it is .00. In contrast, the coefficient for the theoretically specified direct path from religious hostility to anti-Semitism is .20.

A second finding is that the historic image of the Jews as Crucifiers plays virtually no independent role in the model at all! It is somewhat influenced by orthodoxy (.16), but not at all by particularism (.00). Furthermore, it has hardly any influence on religious hostility (.04) and none at all directly on anti-Semitism (.00). This is not to say it is irrelevant. Clearly, such an imagery is an intrinsic part of religious hostility. But, in and of itself, it has virtually no consequences. For many Christians it is meaningless ancient history. What matters is the religious condition of modern Jews, as measured by the Religious Hostility Index. Thus, church pronouncements exonerating the ancient Jews will not reduce the anti-Semitism of Christians unless they are coupled with an attack on notions of the contemporary Jew as damned and an object of divine retribution.

The figure also shows that religious hostility is the joint product of orthodoxy and particularism. Each has roughly the same independent effect on religious hostility (.27 and .25, respectively). Thus, muting particularism would do much to reduce religious hostility, but considerable religious hostility would continue to be directly generated by orthodoxy. This is the same conclusion as that based on tabular analysis.

The path analysis provides strong confirmation of the model of the religious sources of anti-Semitism among laymen as developed in the earlier study. The main paths in which we took theoretical interest and which were sustained by the tabular analysis produce sizable coefficients. Those we rejected—for example, all linkages between the various factors and anti-Semitism, except through religious hostility—yield very small or nonexistent coefficients.[10]

Path Analysis: The Clergy Sample

Following identical techniques,[11] a path analysis was computed on the clergyman sample and is shown in Figure 4. With one exception, which will be discussed below, the relative differences between paths is identical with that among laymen. However, as we reported earlier on the basis of the tabular analysis, the model is stronger among the clergy than the laity. Thus, while the normalized regression coefficient for the direct path from religious hostility to anti-Semitism among laymen is .20, among the clergy it is considerably higher: .30. The effects of the historic image of the Jews as Crucifiers are also stronger in all instances among the clergy than the laity, but the independent role of this factor remains very modest among the clergy, too, as we would expect.

Figure 4. PATH ANALYSIS (CLERGY SAMPLE)

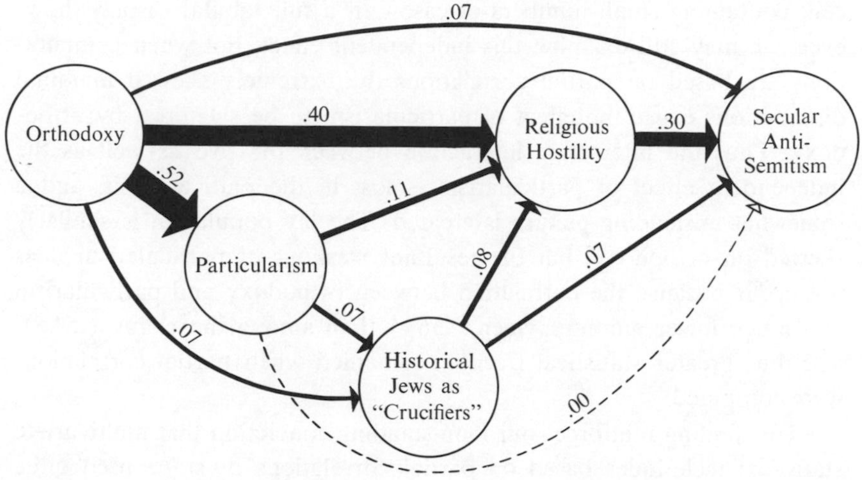

Numbers refer to normalized regression coefficients.
Arrows indicate causal order and are proportional to the coefficients.

The major discrepancy between the two figures concerns the effect of particularism. While the independent effect of particularism on religious hostility was approximately equal to that of orthodoxy among laymen, among the clergy orthodoxy far outweighs particularism. Thus, the coefficient for the direct path from orthodoxy to religious hostility among the clergy is a powerful .40, while that for particularism→religious hostility is only .11.

This apparent discrepancy reflects in part inherent limitations in path analysis and of all multivariate techniques which are based on partial correlations. Recalling Table 15, it has already been seen that particularism has a strong independent effect on religious hostility in all categories of orthodoxy, while the effects of orthodoxy are mainly limited to those high on particularism. This is quite different from what the path analysis shows. The reason lies in the extent to which the distribution of clergymen on the Orthodoxy Index is skewed to the high end. Thus, more than a third of the entire sample scored High on orthodoxy. Of these only 1 scored Low on particularism, only 13 scored Medium, and 511 scored High. This corner cell in the table, which contains a third of the sample, was also marked by an extraordinary amount of religious hostility vis-à-vis other cells in the table. Conversely, the clear pattern of an independent particularism effect is mainly based on cells containing small numbers of cases. In a full tabular display, however, we may still examine this independent effect, but when computations are based on partial correlations the extremely skewed marginal distributions cause the effect of particularism to be swamped by orthodoxy. Thus the interesting interaction between the two as well as the independent effect of particularism is lost in the path analysis, and a somewhat misleading picture is created. The lay population is similarly skewed on orthodoxy, but the resultant washout of particularism does not occur because the correlation between orthodoxy and particularism was much lower among laymen (.364) than among the clergy (.516), and thus greater statistical freedom remained when partial correlations were computed.

This finding reinforces our long-standing conviction that multivariate statistical techniques based on partial correlations must be used quite cautiously in survey analysis. They ought not to be used except in combination with careful tabular analysis.

These reservations notwithstanding, the path analysis does provide a useful summary and depiction of our main findings. Aside from the discrepancy on the power of particularism, a comparison of the two figures shows that the process leading from Christian doctrines to anti-Semitism applies to the clergy as well as the laity. Indeed, although the clergy are less likely than the laity to be anti-Semitic, a larger proportion of their anti-Semitism is rooted in these religious factors.

This raises serious questions about what can be expected of the churches in overcoming the problem of anti-Semitism. Indeed, the present findings raise the even broader question of what can realistically be expected of the clergy as guides on ethical and moral problems in general. This led us to further analysis of the data and resulted in the final chapter.

A Note on Spuriousness

In survey analysis one is always faced with the possibility that the correlations found between variables may be spurious, that is, relationships may be artifacts of some uncontrolled variable. For example, there is a strong correlation between the number of fire trucks at a blaze and the amount of damage sustained. Obviously, fire trucks are not causing the damage. Both are consequences of the size of the fire. When the size of fires is controlled, the original correlation vanishes.

To guard against offering results which are spurious, survey analysts introduce controls for theoretically revelant variables into their analysis. An entire chapter of *Christian Beliefs and Anti-Semitism* was devoted to checking to see whether other plausible variables could, in fact, eliminate the correlations found between the various major elements in the model. Such variables as social class, sex, age, political preference, regional origins, and the like were tested. None reduced the original relationships between religious factors and anti-Semitism. In a sample made up entirely of clergymen, some of these variables are irrelevant as controls. All were males, 94 per cent were college graduates, and 91 per cent were seminary-trained. But other possible sources of spuriousness were tested. Among these were age, region of origin, political preference, and social class origins. Each was found to be related to doctrinalism, religious hostility, and anti-Semitism. The older, more politically conservative clergy from rural and southern and blue-collar origins were more doctrinally conservative and more anti-Semitic. But *none* of these controls produced *any reduction* in the relationships reported in this study. Young ministers who had urban, northern, upper-class origins and favored the Democratic party, *if* they accepted traditional Christian teachings, were just as likely to be religiously hostile and to be anti-Semitic as were their opposite numbers. No variable available in the data which seemed a plausible source of spuriousness was found to be one. In consequence, we must provisionally conclude that the relationships reflect a set of causal connections.

5

Ministers as Moral Guides:
The Silent Majority

A major theme in contemporary writing about the churches is their *potential* for creating brotherhood, social justice, and a more humane society. Frequently the churches have been likened to a sleeping giant; with their vast membership and their presumed moral authority, it is assumed that if the churches roused themselves they could be a potent social force. We are among those who have written and spoken of the churches in such terms. For one thing, our data have shown that the persons who most need their prejudices and complacency shaken are those who are most likely to be in church on Sunday morning. This, we felt, provided the churches with a unique opportunity. At the same time, however, we have been uneasy about this line of thought. Why has the influence of religious institutions remained only potential for so long? Why is it that those who gather in the churches have not had their prejudices shaken to the same extent as those who spend Sunday mornings reading the newspaper and watching the pro football game of the week on television? Is the giant really sleeping or is he too feeble to move?

There have been a number of signs recently that, in fact, the churches cannot do much more than they have been doing, and in light of this evidence perhaps the notion that the churches can rouse themselves to make a major contribution to the human condition is a pious hope. Studies by Jeffrey K. Hadden and others suggest that clergy who have attempted to lead their congregations in the path of an active application of Christian ethics have met fierce resistance. Many have lost their jobs; others have lost heart and left the clergy.[1] Recent studies by Milton Rokeach have strongly confirmed and extended our earlier finding that commitment to Christian orthodoxy tends to be incompatible with commitment to Christian ethical concerns.[2] Rokeach identified two main themes in Christian commitment which he called salvationalism and forgiveness. In principle, each is a necessary component of true Christian orthodoxy; yet he found they tended to be mutually exclusive religious outlooks. Christian concern with personal salvation seems to dry up the capacity for sympathizing with the condition of others. Finally, the previous two chapters show that it was probably unrealistic to look to the churches for vigorous action to combat member anti-Semitism. If the model of the religious roots of anti-Semitism is as applicable to the clergy as to the laity, from where in religious institutions can such vigorous action be expected to come?

Consequently, we are more pessimistic today about the change-producing potential of the churches than two of us were when we wrote the concluding chapter of *Christian Beliefs and Anti-Semitism*. Given that nearly all denominations had condemned the notion of continuing Jewish guilt, it was felt that the effect of that study would be to arouse the clergy to the unfortunate fact that their most committed lay members still clung to what were officially "false doctrines." But roughly the same proportion of clergy also hold these "false" doctrines. If they have not yet healed themselves, how can they be effective physicians?

Such concerns prompted the analysis reported in this chapter. How are the clergy fulfilling their role as shepherds? What efforts are they making to provide guidance to their congregations on the great moral and ethical questions which beset us? And what factors affect how ministers guide their flocks?

The Sounds of Silence

At least once a week pastors are preachers. For the churches the Sunday morning worship service is the primary manifestation of religious activity, and the center of the service is the sermon. The sermon is the primary means whereby the churches, through the clergy, instruct the faithful in the meaning and character of Christian thought. In terms of reaching the laity, the sermon far surpasses other media such as church periodicals, discussion groups, or radio and television programs.[3] Most church members attend church fairly often and in so doing become a captive audience for their pastor's message.

Given the extent of "unchristian" beliefs and attitudes prevalent among those who attend church, some have suggested that the sermon is not an effective means of moral and ethical communication. Many clergy say in despair that sermons seem to fall on deaf ears: people are able to compartmentalize their lives so that their prejudice, hatred, selfishness, and "sinfulness" remain unaffected by messages from the pulpit. But there is a second logical possibility: that the laity remain apparently unshaken by years of sermonizing because rarely does the sermon touch on controversial moral and ethical issues. Have the clergy been trying to lead and failing to achieve results, or are congregations unmoved because the clergy have not made any appreciable efforts to move them?

Thus far very little has been known systematically about what use the clergy make of their sermons. Probably the most accurate way to find out what the clergy are saying from the pulpit would be to assign a group of trained observer-reporters to attend a random sample of church services and record what is said. Of course, this would be a very expensive undertaking. However, it seems reasonable to ask the clergy themselves about the kinds of sermons they give. We recognize that such a technique could produce inflated estimates: that there may be a tendency for clergymen to report sermons they wish they had preached along with those they did preach. Still, as will be considered in detail later, the rationale by which clergymen conduct themselves in the pulpit suggests they do what they think they ought to do and thus should not be self-conscious about sins of omission.

In this section we shall scrutinize clergy reports of whether and how frequently they preach on the great moral and social issues which beset modern society. We shall not be concerned with what stand the clergy have taken on such issues, but only with whether or not they have had anything to say at all.

Table 23 examines clergy performance on three questions dealing with preaching on social and political issues. The first item makes it

Table 23. THE DELIVERY OF SERMONS ON CONTROVERSIAL SOCIAL OR POLITICAL TOPICS

	United Church of Christ	Metho-dist	Epis-copal	Presby-terian	Luth. Church in Amer.	Amer. Luth. Church	American Baptist	Mis-souri Lutheran	South. Baptist	Total
Number	(137)	(354)	(207)	(226)	(87)	(118)	(147)	(134)	(170)	(1,580)
Per cent who *dealt mainly* with a controversial social or political topic										
8 or more times	20%	17%	19%	10%	13%	9%	10%	3%	6%	13%
5–7 times	18	16	14	17	17	5	6	5	3	12
3–4 times	22	32	24	30	21	9	26	10	15	23
Once or twice	24	24	26	29	28	25	32	26	34	27
Never	16	10	17	13	21	52	26	56	42	25
	100%	99%ᵃ	100%	99%ᵃ	100%	100%	100%	100%	100%	100%
Per cent who *touched upon,* but did not deal mainly with, a controversial social or political topic										
8 or more times	56%	67%	60%	57%	68%	42%	50%	38%	35%	54%
5–7 times	11	13	11	20	10	16	18	24	15	15
3–4 times	23	13	16	19	7	21	19	21	19	17
Once or twice	7	5	9	3	9	16	8	9	26	10
Never	3	2	3	1	3	5	5	8	5	4
	100%	100%	99%ᵃ	100%	99%ᵃ	100%	100%	100%	100%	100%
Per cent who have *ever* taken a stand from the pulpit on some political *issue*										
Yesᵇ	72%	81%	64%	69%	63%	38%	33%	26%	47%	62%
No	28	19	36	31	37	62	67	74	53	38
	100%	100%	100%	100%	100%	100%	100%	100%	100%	100%

ᵃ Percentages fail to add to 100 because of rounding error.
ᵇ *Yes* combines "Yes, while in present church," "Yes, before present church," and "Yes, both present church and before."

clear that giving sermons which deal *mainly* with controversial social or political topics is not the usual practice of the clergy. For every minister who reported having given such a sermon at least eight times in the past year (13 per cent), two other clergymen said they had not even given one such sermon (25 per cent). The majority came closer to their totally silent colleagues than to those who devoted one out of six of their approximately forty-eight sermons during the year to controversial social and political topics. Twenty-seven per cent reported giving one or two such sermons, 23 per cent reported giving three or four, and 12 per cent said they had done so five to seven times. Thus, 52 per cent had given no more than two such sermons, and half of these had given none. Based on these self-reports, we calculate that approximately *6 per cent of the sermons given in California Protestant churches during the year preceding the study were mainly devoted to social and political topics.*[4]

Speaking out from the pulpit on such matters is strongly influenced by denomination: while 33 per cent of the Methodists and Episcopalians preached on controversial social and political topics five times or more during the previous year, only 8 per cent of the Missouri Lutherans and 9 per cent of the Southern Baptists did so. Conversely, only 10 per cent of the Methodists failed to give even one such sermon, while 56 per cent of the Missouri Lutherans, 52 per cent of the American Lutheran Church clergy, and 42 per cent of the Southern Baptists found no occasion during the year to devote a sermon to such matters.

In order adequately to gauge the meaning of the fact that only 6 per cent of Protestant sermonizing was devoted to social and political topics during the past year, it is important to recall that this period—late spring, 1967, to late spring, 1968—was one of the most agonizing years in American history. During the summer of 1967 Detroit and dozens of other American cities burned. The Kerner Commission was appointed, conducted investigations, and issued its monumental report on the racial crisis. In Vietnam came the crisis of the Tet offensive, while at home protest against the war became increasingly militant. The McCarthy campaign was launched. Lyndon Johnson announced his withdrawal from the presidential race and began an effort to negotiate peace. The Middle East was torn by the lightning war and followed by a bleeding peace. Biafrans starved by the tens of thousands. In Memphis, the Reverend Dr. Martin Luther King, Jr., was gunned down, and a new wave of riots followed.

In response to these crises, prominent clergy saw profound moral issues and took active roles. Such activists were admittedly only a handful of the whole clergy.[5] But one might have thought their less visible colleagues would have been prompted at least to speak out from the pulpit.

To a limited extent they were. While the many crises were often insufficient to lead pastors to devote the major portion of a sermon to social and political questions, few found it possible to ignore them utterly. As the second item in Table 23 shows, when asked how frequently during the past year they had delivered "sermons which *touched upon,* but did not deal mainly with, controversial social or political topics," only 4 per cent reported never having done so. On the other hand, 54 per cent reported they had done so eight or more times during the year. Clearly, it is relatively more common for the clergy to deal with such matters in a peripheral way than to make them the central topic of a sermon.

The data from questions 1 and 2 tell us nothing, however, about *what is said* when the clergy do choose to speak out from the pulpit. Considering responses to the next item, it is clear that often the clergy speak only in bland, ambiguous, and vague ways on such topics. Item 3 shows the proportion of clergymen who have ever in their entire career taken a stand on a political *issue* from the pulpit. While 62 per cent say they have done so at least once in their lives, more than a third indicate they have *never* made their own position clear from the pulpit on a political *issue.* (We stress *issue*—it was also italicized in the questionnaire —to avoid confusion with taking stands on political candidates, a practice one would not expect to be widespread among the clergy. Political issues, obviously, include such matters as school prayers, legislation on drugs, sexual conduct, divorce, pornography, and the like, not merely party issues. Further, political issues permit conservative as well as liberal comment.) The 62 per cent of the clergy who have taken a stand from the pulpit is considerably smaller than the 96 per cent who report they touched upon a controversial social or political topic in a sermon during the previous year. It is also smaller than the proportion (75 per cent) who said they had devoted at least one sermon mainly to such a topic during the year. From these discrepancies it seems obvious that many clergymen manage to take up a controversial topic from the pulpit without revealing their own moral or ethical positions—to mention controversy without being at all controversial themselves.

Thus, even the relatively poor quantitative performance of the clergy in speaking out from the pulpit must be taken with considerable qualitative reservation. Many who say something say it very circumspectly.

Ministers in conservative denominations are particularly prone to circumspection. For example, while 44 per cent of the Missouri Lutherans say they have preached on a controversial social or political topic in the past year, only 26 per cent say they have ever taken a stand on such an issue. The same comparison among Southern Baptists is 58 and 47 per cent.

In the next section we shall seek to understand why the clergy are so prone to pulpit silence. But first it will be useful to understand when the silence is broken. On the few occasions when more than a handful of the clergy do speak out, what particular social and political issues do they address?

Our findings are that it requires an issue of extraordinary urgency to break the pulpit silence. Even then a substantial proportion of pulpits remain silent.

In the spring of 1968 the issue which most troubled Americans was the war in Vietnam. Thousands of American youth had felt morally obligated to risk prison or leave the country rather than fight and thousands of other Americans risked jail to protest against the war. Bitter controversy raged over the Christian view of the war. The late Cardinal Spellman and others saw it as a holy and Christian endeavor. Other Christian spokesmen saw the war as morally abhorrent.

Among the rank-and-file clergymen the war was sufficiently important to two-thirds of them to be mentioned from the pulpit; 65 per cent said they had *sometime devoted at least one sermon or part of a sermon to the war* (Table 24). For the remaining third, not even the war could break their silence. As was seen with Table 23, silence was more common in the conservative than in the theologically more liberal denominations. While 22 per cent of the Methodist clergy had never mentioned the war from the pulpit, half or more of the American and Missouri Lutherans and Southern Baptists had been mute on the war.

Table 24. THE DELIVERY OF SERMONS ON TWO CONTROVERSIAL ISSUES

	United Church of Christ	Methodist	Episcopal	Presbyterian	Luth. Church in Amer.	Amer. Luth. Church	American Baptist	Missouri Lutheran	South. Baptist	Total
Number	(137)	(354)	(207)	(226)	(87)	(118)	(147)	(134)	(170)	(1,580)
Per cent who had delivered a sermon or a section of a sermon on:										
The Vietnam War	75	78	68	68	69	47	62	47	50	65
Proposition 14	61	79	71	67	63	32	47	22	16	56[a]

[a] Percentages are based on those ministers who were serving California parishes during the time of the Proposition 14 campaign.

If the Vietnam war was the most compelling national issue at the time of the study, the most debated local issue in California was Proposition 14. This was an amendment placed on the ballot to change the constitution of the state in order to repeal an open housing law passed by the legislature and to outlaw any such laws in the future. The amendment was strongly opposed by major political spokesmen from both parties and brought an outpouring of clergy opposition unprecedented in recent California history. Newspapers ran a great many ads opposing the proposition which were signed by most of the prominent church leaders—not only clerical activists but also bishops and denominational leaders not noted for public participation in social issues. (Such moral leadership was repudiated two to one at the polls as the voters abolished the open housing law; the amendment was later voided by the courts.)

So high a degree of public activity by religious leaders had its effect on the parish clergy: a majority who served California parishes at the time of the election delivered a sermon or at least a section of a sermon on this issue. But the majority was hardly overwhelming—56 per cent—while from the remainder of the pulpits silence reigned. Keep in mind that the distinction here is not between being for or against Proposition 14, but between having or not having anything to say about it at all. Again silence is strongly related to denomination; 79 per cent of the Methodists spoke out, while only 22 per cent of the Missouri Lutherans and 16 per cent of the Southern Baptists did so.

The war and Proposition 14 are exceptions that may prove the rule. Of the many other issues we investigated, the majority (and usually the overwhelming majority) of the clergy had not found an occasion during the year to devote a major portion of a sermon to any of them. This is especially remarkable, since the racial problem was one of these topics.

Each clergyman was asked to indicate for each of thirteen issues whether or not during the past year he had preached a sermon which dealt mainly with this topic.

As mentioned earlier, the past year in question was one of racial trauma, beginning with fire and death in Detroit and many other cities and ending with the assassination of Martin Luther King, Jr. Thus, it is no surprise that "racial problems" led the list among these thirteen topics on which sermons had been preached. Rather the surprise lies in the fact that the majority of pulpits (55 per cent) had not been used for such a sermon: *the majority of Protestant clergymen in California— not in Mississippi or North Dakota—had not devoted a single sermon mainly to racial problems during this year of death, turmoil, and tragedy.*

From racial problems on, the extent of sermonizing on social problems declined rapidly to near nonexistence:[6]

— Only 28 per cent preached on World Poverty, while a mere 22 per cent preached on National Poverty.
— Crime and Juvenile Delinquency sermons were given from one of five Protestant pulpits in California.
— 16 per cent delivered sermons on The UN and World Peace.
— Drugs, alcohol, and sex were preached about by 14 to 16 per cent of the clergy.
— Black Power (7 per cent), Birth Control (3 per cent), Capital Punishment (8 per cent), and The Conduct of Public Officials (5 per cent) received mention from only a tiny proportion of pulpits.
— Only 2 per cent preached on Abortion Laws, despite the fact that this was a widely disputed issue at the time.[7]

Given the fact that the average minister in this sample devoted only three sermons during the year mainly to social and political issues, it is no surprise that these specific topics were so infrequently taken up. Yet the silence itself remains enigmatic. It is as if there had been no Sermon on the Mount. In the next section we shall try to determine why so many clergymen act as if Christian doctrine has no implications for human suffering and social abominations. But whatever the reasons, these data dispel the notion that it is the deaf ears of the laity which account for their apparent apathy and tolerance of injustice. They cannot be blamed for ignoring sermons that were not preached. Indeed, if the laity appear to be deaf to the voice of the clergy, it may be because they found the silence deafening.

The Sources of Silence

Most pulpits are silent. Why?

To answer this question is also to say why some clergymen, albeit a

Table 25. DOCTRINALISM AND SPEAKING OUT ON SOCIAL AND POLITICAL ISSUES

	Doctrinal Index					
	Low				High	
	0	· 1	2	3	4	Total
Number	(28)	(134)	(296)	(467)	(568)	(1,493)
1. Per cent who have *ever* taken a stand from the pulpit on some political issue	93	80	79	67	42	62
2. *"During the past year, how often did you deliver sermons which dealt mainly with controversial social or political topics?"*						
Per cent who did so at least *five* times	66	40	38	26	10	25
Per cent who *never* did so	0	7	11	18	42	25
3. *"During the past year, how often did you deliver sermons which touched upon, but did not deal mainly with, controversial social or political topics?"*						
Per cent who did so at least *five* times	88	82	78	73	54	68
Per cent who *never* did so	0	0	1	3	7	4
4. Per cent who *ever* delivered a sermon *or a section* of a sermon on:						
Proposition 14	95	80	74	65	29	56[a]
The War in Vietnam	89	80	75	69	49	65
5. Per cent who gave a sermon *during the previous year* which dealt mainly with:						
Racial Problems	78	66	63	53	25	45
World Poverty	52	41	33	34	18	28
National Poverty	68	36	25	29	12	22
The UN and World Peace	33	27	30	18	6	16
Capital Punishment	19	18	10	8	4	8
Black Power	22	18	12	7	3	7
The Conduct of Public Officials	15	6	4	5	5	5
Birth Control	19	2	5	2	1	3
Abortion Laws	19	4	3	2	1	2
Crime and Juvenile Delinquency	30	18	18	19	24	20
The Use of Drugs	26	15	13	13	16	14
Alcoholism	19	11	13	14	17	14
Sexual Conduct	15	12	15	19	18	16

[a] Based only on those ministers serving California parishes at the time of the Proposition 14 issue.

minority, do speak out on the moral, social, and political issues that divide and anguish Americans.

Past speculation and writing on this question have concentrated on character defects of individual clergymen, such as their timidity, and on the hostility of the social climate in which they perform.[8] But a forthcoming volume based on these same data indicates that these are at best marginal factors influencing the clergy.[9] The overwhelming majority of clergymen in all denominations believe in the power of the pulpit and thus reject the "deaf ears cause frustration" explanation of pulpit silence. Yet many do not use this power. All sectors of the clergy believe that their congregations object to "relevant" sermons. But some give them anyway. There is some evidence that clergymen who believe their colleagues approve of speaking out are more likely to do so. But the effect is not large and is modified by the fact that those who believe their colleagues would not approve of such behavior do not themselves approve of clergymen speaking out. Thus, it is difficult to attribute their silence to conformity with the expectations of fellow clergymen. It could just as easily be conformity to their own conceptions of propriety.

Consequently our search for the sources of silence turned elsewhere. In examining the data we became convinced that pulpit silence is not something imposed on the clergy, but something they impose on themselves; that just as much as the clergyman who speaks out believes in what he is doing, so the clergyman who remains silent believes he is doing the right thing. And each bases his interpretation on his theological, social, and political beliefs.

We begin with the theological roots of silence. Table 25 shows the relationship between the many items on pulpit behavior we have examined in this chapter and a modified form of the Doctrinalism Index used in previous chapters.[10] The relationships are very strong: the more doctrinally conservative, the less likely a minister is to speak out. Thus, 93 per cent of those who scored zero on doctrinalism have at some time (at least once) taken a stand from the pulpit on some political issue, while only 42 per cent of the most conservative have ever done so. Sixty-six per cent of the least theologically conservative had preached on controversial topics five times or more in the past year, and only 10 per cent of the most conservative had done so. Indeed, nearly half (42 per cent) of the most conservative had never done so, and only half of them (54 per cent) had even "touched upon" such topics in one sermon out of ten during the last year.

When we come to specific issues the pattern remains much the same. Virtually all those who scored zero and 80 per cent of those who scored 1 on doctrinalism preached on Proposition 14—the referendum to repeal an open housing law—while only 29 per cent of those who scored 4 did so. Nine out of ten of the liberals had preached on the war; five out of ten of the most conservative clergy had not. On racial problems, three-fourths of those who scored zero and two-thirds of those who scored 1 gave at least one sermon out of forty-eight which dealt mainly with racial problems, while three-fourths of those who scored 4 did not. And thus it goes until the last four items (below the broken line in the table).

While on all other sermon topics in the table there was a strong, linear, negative relationship between doctrinalism and preaching on social and political issues, on these four items this pattern gives way to curvilinear relationships. On the issues of Crime and Juvenile Delinquency, The Use of Drugs, Alcoholism, and Sexual Conduct there is a tendency for the most and least doctrinally committed to be the two groups most likely to have preached about them. That is, reading across these items from left to right, the proportions tend to fall as doctrinal scores increase and then to reverse the trend and climb again.

When we recognize that each of these topics concerns not only social and political issues but "personal vices" in the most traditional sense, the reasons for this curvilinearity become apparent. Traditional Christianity has placed major emphasis on combating personal vices, which are defined as barriers to salvation. Indeed, a major criticism made of evangelical Christianity by liberal Christian spokesmen is the privatism and egocentricism of this inclination to define morality in purely individualistic and vice terms.[11] Thus, it should not occasion surprise that the more conservative clergy mention such topics from the pulpit; perhaps it is more surprising that they are generally so unlikely to do so. Presumably, when the liberal clergy preach on these topics they tend to do so in terms of a social problems perspective rather than in terms of individual sin. We also suspect that when the conservative clergy preach on such topics it is to denounce such individual action—that the conservatives, for example, emphasize "Thou shalt not steal" when they preach on crime, while the more liberal clergy emphasize the social causes of crime.

Support for this interpretation can be found in the fact that an overwhelming 82 per cent of those who scored zero on doctrinalism advocated *weakening* the laws regulating marijuana, while an equally overwhelming 78 per cent of those who scored 4 wanted to make these laws *stronger*. Similarly, only 18 per cent of those who scored zero wanted to strengthen laws regulating the sale of liquor (more than wanted to strengthen laws against marijuana), while 65 per cent of those who scored 4 wanted to strengthen such laws. Clearly, sermons on drugs and liquor by groups holding such opposite views would be very different indeed.

Thus we have seen that theological convictions, as measured by the Doctrinal Index, strongly influence pulpit performance. It seems obvious that theology would influence the content of what is said on social and political issues. But that is not presently at issue. *Why does theology so powerfully influence the very act of speaking out?* It is inadequate to rest our exploration of theological sources of silence simply with these findings. To say silence is produced by conservative theology is simply to deepen the mystery. The Sermon on the Mount is also a part of traditional Christianity. We must know what it is about traditional doctrines that disposes the conservative clergy to remain silent.

A first step toward understanding the role of theology in pulpit silence is to see how it affects conceptions of what sermons are for. The clergymen were asked, "How important do you feel it is to accomplish each of the following purposes in your sermons?" The findings appear in Table 26. The first of these sermon purposes—"point out the existence of human sin"—deals directly with the differences we have already observed on sermon topics. While only 32 per cent of those who scored zero and 24 per cent of those who scored 1 on doctrinalism felt this was very important, 77 per cent of those who scored 4 did so. It would be quite possible to interpret speaking out on political and social issues as pointing out human sin, but from these data one must conclude that the clergy did not regard this item from such a frame of reference. The fact that it is the conservatives who feel this is important (and who remain silent on social and political matters), and the liberals (who speak out) who regard this as unimportant, suggests that this item was understood primarily as sin in the old-fashioned hell-fire sense.

Table 26.   DOCTRINALISM AND THE PURPOSE OF SERMONS

			Doctrinal Index			
Number	Low 0 (28)	1 (134)	2 (296)	3 (467)	High 4 (568)	Total (1,493)
"How important do you feel it is to accomplish each of the following purposes in your sermons?"						
Per cent who thought it very important to "point out the existence of human sin."	32	24	33	49	77	54
Per cent who thought it very important to "illustrate the type of life a Christian should follow."	57	63	78	76	89	79
Per cent who thought it very important to "apply Christian standards to judge human institutions and behavior."	72	75	75	69	73	73
Per cent who thought it very important to provide "spiritual uplifting and moral comfort."	39	55	68	69	87	74

The second item—"illustrate the type of life a Christian should follow"—is closely related to the first, and eight out of ten clergymen felt it very important to accomplish this in their sermons. On this item a majority of liberals join with an overwhelming majority of conservatives (although a substantial relationship still remains). But clearly liberals and conservatives read this item differently. Since the conservatives are very unlikely to preach on social and political topics, they must define a Christian type of life on rather different criteria than do the liberals. This is further corroborated by the answers to the third item. Nearly three-fourths of the clergy (73 per cent) agreed it is very important that a sermon "apply Christian standards to judge human institutions and behavior." Responses here are not affected by doctrinalism. But since we know that the liberals do preach about human institutions and conservatives rarely or never seem to do so, it seems certain that there is substantial disagreement over how this purpose of sermons is to be accomplished. Apparently, in the judgment of conservatives this is done by preaching on the weaknesses of the flesh.

Finally, we see that doctrinalism is powerfully related to what has been called the "comforting function" of religion.[12] The last item reflects this in relatively pure form: to provide "spiritual uplifting and moral comfort to those who are distressed." Most conservatives thought this was very important to accomplish in their sermons. Among those least doctrinally conservative, most did not.

Looking back over these items, it seems clear that conservatives tend to view the purpose of their sermons in terms of individual salvation and sin. And they define both in a relatively otherworldly way. Human sin, apparently, is not predominantly related to social and political issues, and salvation does not, for example, seem to depend on freeing oneself of prejudice. We shall now follow up these cues directly.

Otherworldliness and the Miracle Motif

One of the critical issues in modern religion is a conflict between a salvational conception of the mission of the church and a this-worldly, direct approach to social ills. There are several major strands to this argument. The first minimizes the importance of this world. Life is merely a time of testing during which one must establish his right to spend eternity in heaven. The proper role of the clergy is to help members ignore the trivial concerns of this world—for all these things shall pass away—and to fix their concern on preparing for life beyond the grave. Furthermore, this conception of what is truly important rejects the possibility of substantially improving worldly affairs. This world is necessarily sinful to the point of depravity, and it is the most sinful sort of human pride to think otherwise. From this point of view, men should concentrate on overcoming their personal vices and committing themselves to Christ's redeeming love. "Where will you spend eternity?" is the only worthwhile concern.

The second strand in the salvational conception of the mission of the church is what two of us elsewhere called the miracle motif.[13]

Recently, in response to critics, Billy Graham claimed to be a revolutionary. He argued that far from being unresponsive to the growing crises in human affairs—war, annihilation, inequality, hatred, and despair —he is actively pursuing a complete reconstruction of society. He believes that he differs with his critics primarily on means, not ends. For Graham, the means are a miraculous revolution through individual salvation. Graham is hardly an isolated instance. Rather the thrust of evangelical Protestantism is toward a miraculous view of social reform: that if all men are brought to Christ, social evils will disappear through the miraculous regeneration of the individual by the Holy Spirit. Thus evangelicals concentrate on conversion, and except for occasional efforts to outlaw what they deem to be personal vices, evangelical Protestant groups largely ignore social and political efforts for reform. Indeed, they also largely ignore the fact that "born-again" and regenerated Christians seem to remain noticeably sinful. Perhaps because they rely on a miracle to change their adherents, they say little about how the miraculously changed man ought to act. A possibly unintended consequence of Christian preoccupation with individual salvation is a suspicion of, and often a hostility to, social and political efforts for reform. So long as there are men who have not been won to Christ, a sinful society is seen as inevitable. Therefore, any attempts to reform society, other than through conversion of individuals to Christ, are doomed to failure.

Theological conceptions such as these could play a substantial role in the silence of the more conservative clergy on social issues. From their perspective it would seem there is nothing to say about such matters that is not said in exhorting men to give their lives to Christ. If "Christ is the answer," why talk about superficialities such as programs to ease social crises?

The more liberal Protestant clergy, of course, strongly reject these otherworldly and miraculous views. They argue that reliance on individual salvation as the sole means for ameliorating social problems is theologically wrong and impractical. Furthermore, they reject the idea that Christian morality and ethics are primarily concerned with the relationship between man and God. Rather they see them as primarily between men and emphasize loving thy neighbor as the major Christian ethical dictum.

We need give no further explication of this theological controversy. Our interest is in whether or not salvational and miraculous orientations remain common among the Christian clergy and whether or not such orientations are responsible for the silence of the clergy on major social issues.

Table 27 shows that such views are widespread, and they are powerfully related to the Doctrinal Index.

Item 1 assesses the miracle motif. Ministers were asked to agree or disagree with the statement: "If enough men were brought to Christ, social ills would take care of themselves." Over all, 44 per cent of the clergy agreed, 42 per cent disagreed, and the rest were uncertain of their position on this question. Thus the clergy are about evenly split on the conception of saving society by saving individual souls. Agreement, as would be expected, is powerfully related to one's religious views as measured by the Doctrinal Index. Seven per cent of the lowest scorers agreed with this statement, while 77 per cent of the highest scorers did so.

The second item contains elements of both otherworldliness and the miracle motif: "It would be better if the church were to place less emphasis on individual sanctification and more on bringing human conditions into conformity with Christian teachings." Again the clergy are about evenly split. Forty-seven per cent agreed that emphasis should shift from individual sanctification to human conditions, while 42 per cent disagreed. And again the relationship with doctrinalism is very powerful: 93 per cent of the lowest scorers agreed, while only 19 per cent of the highest scorers did so.

The final item is a fairly extreme assessment of otherworldliness: "It is not as important to worry about life after death as about what one can do in this life." Two-thirds of the clergy accepted this statement and thus put this world ahead of the world to come. Still, the relationship with doctrinalism remains very powerful. While *every* clergyman who scored zero on the Doctrinalism Index agreed with this statement, only 42 per cent of those who scored highest did so.

Table 27.   DOCTRINALISM, OTHERWORLDLINESS, AND THE MIRACLE MOTIF

| | | | Doctrinal Index | | | |
	Low 0 (28)	1 (134)	2 (296)	3 (467)	High 4 (568)	Total (1,493)
Number						
1. *"If enough men were brought to Christ, social ills would take care of themselves."*						
Per cent agree	7	17	35	41	77	44
Per cent disagree	86	69	54	51	21	42
2. *"It would be better if the church were to place less emphasis on individual sanctification and more on bringing human conditions into conformity with Christian teachings."*						
Per cent agree	93	80	73	51	19	47
Per cent disagree	4	11	18	36	69	42
3. *"It is not as important to worry about life after death as about what one can do in this life."*						
Per cent agree	100	93	90	76	42	68
Per cent disagree	0	6	7	19	47	26

Based on these findings, it is plain that the more traditional clergy tend to have an antipathy toward the affairs of this world and to believe that individual salvation will solve our social ills. Is it any wonder that they do not preach on social problems? Tables 28, 29, and 30 indicate that it is not.

If an important reason for the silence of the doctrinally conservative clergy is their commitment to miraculous and otherworldly solutions to human problems, the strong original relationships between doctrinalism and preaching on various topics ought to be substantially reduced when such otherworldliness is controlled. We do not hypothesize that this is the only linking mechanism involved, but we do hypothesize that it is an important mechanism. Thus, the reductions of the original relationship should be quite sizable, if our hypothesis is correct.

The logic of this argument is that an important reason why clergymen do not address themselves to social issues in their sermons lies not merely in their commitment to traditional church doctrines, but that such doctrinal commitment leads them also to adopt an otherworldly, miraculous outlook, and this in turn makes preaching on such issues seem irrelevant.

Table 28.   DOCTRINALISM, OTHERWORLDLINESS, AND PREACHING ON POLITICAL ISSUES

(Per cent who have *never* taken a stand from the pulpit on some political issue.)

	Doctrinal Index					Correlation coefficients[a] within categories of otherworldliness
	Low				High	
	0	1	2	3	4	DXY
Otherworldliness Index:						
None	0	0	0	—	X	−.064
Number	(6)	(8)	(12)	(9)		
Low	11	13	13	27	48	.138
Number	(18)	(85)	(151)	(151)	(42)	
Medium	0	57	33	36	51	.110
Number	(1)	(14)	(61)	(162)	(182)	
High	X	—	—	54	64	.049
Number		(1)	(9)	(46)	(231)	
Original relationship	7	19	21	33	58	Original correlation coefficient .237

ᵃ Somers' DXY.

To test empirically these suppositions, an Otherworldliness Index was constructed from the three items discussed above and shown in Table 25. Scores on the index range from none (persons who rejected all otherworldliness items) to high (those who embraced all otherworldliness items).[14] We then used this index as a control on several of the key relationships previously presented in Table 25. The results are shown in Tables 28–30.

Looking first at Table 28, it is apparent that in categories of the Otherworldliness Index the powerful original relationship between doctrinalism and *never* having taken a stand from the pulpit on some political issue is substantially reduced, that is, the percentage-point differences between lower and higher scorers on doctrinalism are smaller when scores on otherworldliness are controlled. This can most readily be seen by comparing correlation coefficients.[15] The correlation between doctrinalism and never taking a stand is .237. When otherworldiness is controlled, the resulting coefficients are reduced considerably, ranging from virtually zero to .138. The amount of the reduction can be interpreted as the extent to which the original relationship is produced by the fact that those committed to traditional Christian doctrines are led to ignore social and political issues from the pulpit *because they believe salvation of the individual is the only relevant solution to such problems.*

Table 29 reveals a similar reduction. Here the original relationship

Table 29.   DOCTRINALISM, OTHERWORLDLINESS, AND GIVING A
CONTROVERSIAL SERMON

(Per cent who during the past year *did not* deliver a sermon which dealt mainly with a controversial social or political topic.)

	Doctrinal Index					Controlled DXY
	Low				High	
	0	1	2	3	4	
Otherworldliness Index:						
None	0	0	8	0	X	.076
Number	(6)	(8)	(12)	(9)		
Low	0	4	6	15	29	.193
Number	(17)	(82)	(146)	(149)	(42)	
Medium	0	14	17	19	34	.208
Number	(1)	(14)	(60)	(159)	(181)	
High	X	0	—	30	53	.248
Number		(1)	(8)	(46)	(231)	
Original						Original DXY
relationship	0	7	11	18	43	.344

between doctrinalism and the proportions who did not deliver a sermon in the past year which dealt mainly with a controversial social or political topic is reexamined with otherworldliness controlled. Within each category of the Otherworldliness Index the relationship is smaller than originally. The original correlation coefficient of .344 declines to .076, .193, .208, and .248 when the control is added. Again, the hypothesis that otherworldliness is the mechanism linking doctrinalism and silence is substantially confirmed.

Table 30. DOCTRINALISM, OTHERWORLDLINESS, AND GIVING A SERMON ON RACIAL PROBLEMS AND ON WORLD POVERTY

(Per cent who during the past year devoted at least one sermon mainly to racial problems.)						Controlled DXY
	Doctrinal Index					
	Low 0	1	2	3	High 4	
Otherworldliness Index:						
None	—	—	67	—	X	.062
Number	(6)	(8)	(12)	(9)		
Low	70	67	69	58	40	.101
Number	(17)	(82)	(145)	(144)	(38)	
Medium	—	57	44	50	30	.146
Number	(1)	(14)	(59)	(154)	(173)	
High	X	0	—	38	19	.223
Number		(1)	(7)	(45)	(211)	
Original						Original DXY
relationship	78	67	63	52	25	.262

(Per cent who during the past year devoted at least one sermon mainly to world poverty.)						Controlled DXY
	Doctrinal Index					
	Low 0	1	2	3	High 4	
Otherworldliness Index:						
None	—	—	50	—	X	.107
Number	(6)	(8)	(12)	(9)		
Low	47	43	35	39	37	.013
Number	(17)	(82)	(145)	(144)	(38)	
Medium	0	29	22	32	21	.010
Number	(1)	(14)	(59)	(154)	(173)	
High	X	0	—	22	13	.160
Number		(1)	(7)	(45)	(211)	
Original						Original DXY
relationship	52	41	33	34	18	.138

Table 30 reexamines sermonizing on two specific problems: race and poverty. In both instances there is a substantial reduction in the original relationship between doctrinalism and preaching on social justice. The correlation between doctrinalism and preaching on racial problems is reduced from .262 to .062, .101, .146, and .223, while on world poverty the reduction is from .138 to .107, .013, .010, and (no reduction) .160.

Thus suspicions that a chain of theological convictions is a primary source of pulpit silence is convincingly sustained statistically. But we do not have to rest our case here. There is strong evidence available that the motives we have imputed to the clergy are recognized and accepted by the clergy themselves. In a sense, we have not uncovered a process which the clergy have failed to recognize, but only one which had not previously been empirically confirmed.

The clergymen in the sample were asked to evaluate various factors which might encourage or discourage individual ministers to "participate in social action activities." Now, admittedly, this is not exactly the same thing as preaching sermons on the questions toward which the social action activities of the clergy are normally directed, although action and preaching are very strongly related.[16] Still, it is very interesting to see in Table 31 how ministers rated their own theological views as affecting

Table 31.   DOCTRINALISM AND THE EFFECT OF CLERGY VIEWS ON SOCIAL ACTION

	Doctrinal Index					
	Low				High	
	0	1	2	3	4	Total
Number	(28)	(134)	(296)	(467)	(568)	(1,493)
Per cent who said their "own *theological views*" generally *encouraged* their participation in social action activities	96	90	84	79	39	67

social action. Over all, two-thirds said that their own theological views *generally encouraged* participation in social action. But while 96 per cent of the least doctrinally committed and 90 per cent of those who scored 1 chose this response, only a minority—39 per cent—of the most conservative clergy did so. This closely parallels the proportions who use their pulpits to speak out on social issues—at least once in a while. It also indicates that the majority of the conservative clergy find some incompatibility between their theological convictions and the appropriateness of participation in social action. We have argued precisely this point and expanded it to include preaching on social and political issues. An excellent test of whether or not we are properly interpreting the implications of Table 31 is relatively simple. If our interpretation is correct, differences among clergy in judging their theological views as encouraging or discouraging their participation in social action can be substituted for the Otherworldliness Index wtih similar consequences. That is, the individual clergyman's own evalution ought to be as effective as that we have imputed to him.

Table 32 shows that this is the case. The clergy's own views are effective replacement controls which reduce the original relationships about as well as the Otherworldliness Index did. Thus, on never taking a stand from the pulpit on a political issue the correlation coefficient is reduced from .237 to .092, .065, and .102 by adding the self-designated control. On preaching a sermon on racial problems in the past year the reduction is from .262 to .140, .145, and .195.

This interchangeability of measures is strong testimony for the validity of our inference of the otherworldly, theological source of clerical silence. We are forced to conclude that a major reason why clergymen high on doctrinalism are so much less likely than their more modernist colleagues to preach about the problems of race, war, or poverty is that they see such problems as mundane in contrast to the joys of the world to come, and besides they believe these social ills would take care of themselves if enough men were brought to Christ.

There remains, however, a perhaps unlikely but nevertheless possible alternative explanation for these findings. It is held in some conservative theological circles and by some denominations that the pulpit ought to be reserved for communicating the Gospel in all its purity and that sermons ought not be derailed from this "sacred" purpose by dealing with more mundane matters of everyday life. The existence of this perspective was indicated earlier, when we examined clergy conceptions of the purposes of sermons. The responses of conservative clergy were considerably more consistent with a purely sacred view of the use of the sermon than were those of the liberal clergy.

Thus, it is conceivable that doctrinally conservative clergymen, while

Table 32.   SUBJECTIVE ASSESSMENT OF ROLE OF THEIR OWN THEOLOGICAL VIEWS
AS A SUBSTITUTE FOR THE OTHERWORLDLINESS INDEX

(Per cent who have *never* taken a stand from the pulpit on some political issue.)

	Doctrinal Index					Controlled DXY
	Low 0	1	2	3	High 4	
Generally encourages their participation:	4	14	15	25	37	.092
Number	(27)	(120)	(249)	(372)	(223)	
Generally discourages their participation:	—	—	60	69	73	.065
Number	(1)	(4)	(25)	(62)	(229)	
Neither:	X	—	47	63	69	.102
Number		(9)	(17)	(32)	(105)	
Original relationship:	7	19	21	33	58	Original DXY .237

(Per cent who during the past year devoted at least one sermon
mainly to racial problems.)

	Doctrinal Index					Controlled DXY
	Low 0	1	2	3	High 4	
Clergy judgments of the effect of their own theological views on their participation in social action activities						
Generally encourages their participation:	78	69	67	60	42	.140
Number	(27)	(117)	(240)	(360)	(214)	
Generally discourages their participation:	0	—	33	22	14	.145
Number	(1)	(4)	(24)	(58)	(209)	
Neither:	X	—	38	23	14	.195
Number		(9)	(16)	(30)	(94)	
Original relationship:	78	67	63	52	25	Original DXY .262

considerably less likely than their more liberal counterparts to speak
out on the moral and social issues of the day in sermons, may be as
likely or even more likely to speak out in other contexts. We were able

to check out this possibility by examining responses to the question, "How frequently do you discuss public affairs with members of your congregation?"

All in all, 54 per cent of the clergy reported that they do this frequently, but the most doctrinally liberal clergy are twice as likely to do so as the most doctrinally conservative clergy. The range between the extremes is from 82 to 41 per cent, figures which are very consistent with those found earlier with reference to clergy performance in the pulpit.

A further indication that the phenomenon we have been examining covers more than pulpit behavior is that the most liberal clergy are also much more likely than the most conservative clergy (64 per cent versus 26 per cent) to say that they feel that they have a special obligation to stay politically informed.

Thus the conclusion is warranted that it is because of their religious convictions that many Protestant clergymen reject the relevance of speaking out from the pulpit or elswhere on social issues. So long as this continues to be the case, it seems futile to expect them to change their pulpit performances. If the majority remain silent, it is because they believe in doing so.

Yet this is not the whole story. While the Otherworldliness Index greatly reduced the original relationship between doctrinalism and preaching on these social issues, some of the original effect remained. We now seek further insights into why these relationships obtain.

Prejudice

We have seen that many clergymen apparently did not use their pulpit for speaking out on racial problems—despite the fact that the time in question was one of extraordinary racial unrest—because they are committed to an otherworldly and miraculous religious outlook which obviates direct concern with social injustice. But this is not the only potential source of silence. It is possible that some of this silence was a result of prejudice and racism. Logically, of course, pastors who are prejudiced against blacks and who oppose integration and liberation could have said so from the pulpit (and perhaps some did; we only know who did and who did not preach on racial problems, not what those who did preach said). But it is also possible that in the current climate of opinion, especially in California, prejudiced ministers are reluctant to speak out. It is also possible that such clergymen, recognizing the prejudice of their laymen, feel there is no need to convince them. Consequently, an examination of clergy attitudes and opinions about racial issues may afford further understanding of their pulpit behavior.

Table 33.   DOCTRINALISM AND RACISM

	Doctrinal Index					
	Low				High	
	0	1	2	3	4	Total
Number	(28)	(134)	(296)	(467)	(568)	(1,493)
"It's probably better for Negroes and whites to have their own separate churches." Per cent disagree	96	92	91	89	67	81
"The black power movement is probably necessary in order for white society to realize the extent of Negro frustrations and deprivations." Per cent disagree	4	9	14	25	56	33
"Black power groups such as the Student Non-Violent Coordinating Committee (SNCC) are doing the Negro cause a disservice in their emphasis on racial conflict and violence." Per cent agree	36	47	58	69	90	71

Perhaps the closest approximation to an acid test for racism among the clergy is the issue of church segregation. It has been accurately said that 11 to 12 A.M. on Sundays is the most segregated hour in American life. The question is, Do clergymen approve of this situation? The first item in Table 33 shows that most do not: 81 per cent disagreed with the statement, "It's probably better for Negroes and whites to have their own separate churches." This is substantial opposition to religious segregation. However, as with most issues we have examined, such opposition is not equally characteristic of all groups of clergy. Thus, while there is virtually unanimous opposition among those with lower scores on the Doctrinalism Index, there is a substantial drop-off among the more conservative, only two-thirds of whom disagreed with the statement. Thus, among those who scored zero on doctrinalism, nineteen of twenty opposed church segregation. Among those with maximum scores of 4, only two in three opposed. Once again it must be remembered that there were only 28 zero scorers, as compared with 568 who scored 4. Thus, there is some racism among the clergy, and it tends to be highly concentrated among those most committed to traditional religious doctrines.

The second item raises the question of black power: "The black power movement is probably necessary in order for white society to realize the extent of Negro frustrations and deprivations." Note that the item does not directly imply approval of the black power movement; it is merely an admission that white unresponsiveness made it necessary. One could well agree with this statement and still wish that alternative methods had sufficed. The majority of the clergy in our sample were willing to agree with this statement. But one-third would not. And these are overwhelmingly those who scored high on the Doctrinal Index: while only 4 per cent of the zeros and 9 per cent of the 1's disagreed, a quarter of those who scored 3 and 56 per cent of those who scored 4 did so.

Moving from a general acceptance of the black power movement as "probably necessary" to a more specific assertion, approval melts away. Item 3 stated: "Black power groups such as the Student Non-Violent Coordinating Committee (SNCC) are doing the Negro cause a disservice in their emphasis on racial conflict and violence." Seventy-one per cent of the clergy agreed that groups such as SNCC were placing emphasis on racial conflict and violence and disapproved of it—that is, agreed with the statement. Furthermore, agreement is again powerfully correlated with doctrinalism: 36 per cent of the zero scores agreed, while 90 per cent of those who scored 4 agreed. It could be argued that the more doctrinally conservative are simply more likely to abhor conflict and violence, in keeping with traditional Christian moral preachments. But this argument seems falsified by the fact that they were much more likely than were those low on doctrinalism to support violence by the police. Two-thirds of them called for "tougher police practices" to put down riots, while fewer than one in ten of the lowest scorers did so. Since the police practices being used against riots commonly included the use of deadly force at the time of the study, tougher practices hardly can have referred to nonviolent toughness. We must conclude that these negative reactions to black violence are greatly influenced by racial attitudes.

Table 34.   THE EFFECT OF RACISM ON PREACHING ON RACIAL PROBLEMS

(Per cent who during the past year devoted at least one sermon mainly to racial problems.)

	Doctrinal Index					Controlled DXY
	Low 0	1	2	3	High 4	
Otherworldliness Index						
Those who scored Low:						
All	70	67	69	58	40	.101
Number	(17)	(82)	(145)	(144)	(38)	
Only those who reject segregrated churches	70	70	68	57	52	.078
Number	(17)	(76)	(138)	(133)	(27)	
Those who scored Medium:						
All	—	57	44	50	30	.146
Number	(1)	(14)	(59)	(154)	(173)	
Only those who rejected segregated churches	—	54	45	51	36	.100
Number	(1)	(13)	(53)	(140)	(125)	
Original relationship	78	67	63	52	25	Original DXY .262

We now turn to the question of whether or not racism enters into the decision of the more traditional clergy not to preach on racial problems. Recalling Table 30, we showed that a commitment to otherworldliness played an important role in linking doctrinalism and not preaching on racial problems. However, some portion of the original relationship between doctrinalism and preaching remained. In Table 34 we reexamine the findings in Table 30, but in addition clergy attitudes on church segregation are also controlled. This control is by exclusion.

For lack of sufficient cases of clergymen who approved of church segregation, the full complexity of the data cannot be shown in tabular form. However, the table does contrast all the clergy (from Table 30) with only those who reject church segregation. As can be seen, controlling for racism does produce a significant further reduction in the relationship between doctrinalism and preaching on racial problems. Removal of clergymen with racist sentiments primarily affects the group most conservative on doctrinalism, for this is where such clergymen are concentrated. With those favoring segregated churches removed, the proportion of very conservative clergymen who did deliver a sermon on racial problems increases, from 40 to 52 per cent among those who scored Low on otherworldliness and from 30 to 36 per cent among those who scored Medium, and, although not shown in the table, from 19 to 24 per cent among those who scored High. Among the most conservative clergy who favored segregated churches, the corresponding proportions who preached on racial problems were 10, 12, and 6 per cent, respectively. A comparison of correlation coefficients also shows a significant further reduction when controls for racism are added: the coefficients drop from .101 to .078 and from .146 to .100. Similar reductions occurred when other measures of racial prejudice were used as controls.

Thus we must face the stubborn fact of racism. A significant number of the clergy hold prejudiced views. Such clergymen are disproportionately concentrated among the doctrinally conservative, and they are also less likely than their equally theologically conservative but unprejudiced colleagues to preach on racial problems. Thus, some of the silence on this issue from the pulpit reflected racism, not simply otherworldliness. However, some with racist views did preach on racial problems.

The data force a further assessment of the meaning of our earlier finding that only 45 per cent of the clergy had preached a sermon mainly on the race issue during this time of racial tension. We thought that number surprisingly low. But we must now also recognize that included among this minority who spoke out were some who believe in segregated churches and the like. For those committed to racial justice, sermons by the clergy are not uniformly an unmixed blessing.

Yet it must be kept clearly in mind that silence from the pulpit on racial issues is mainly a theological, not racist, consequence. On the other hand, theology is not all. It will have become increasingly clear in previous discussions that the more modernist clergy are not only more likely to speak out on social and political issues but also more likely to hold liberal views on these issues. And the data showed that political liberalism in and of itself affects the propensity to speak out. These findings will be presented in detail in another volume.[17] We shall only touch upon them here and then consider their implications for the future of the churches.

Theological liberalism, as measured by the Doctrinalism Index, was consistently and powerfully related to a host of liberal political and social views. Such liberalism, in turn, was strongly related to behavior both in and out of the pulpit. Thus, clergymen who opposed the repeal of open housing were much more likely to preach on the issue (68 per cent did) than were those who favored repeal (16 per cent did). Clergymen who advocated military withdrawal from Vietnam were very likely to preach on the war (81 per cent did), while those who favored continued bombing were less likely to preach (60 per cent), and those who favored military escalation as a solution were least likely to have devoted even part of a sermon to the war (49 per cent). Similarly, clergymen with the most liberal economic attitudes were those most likely to have preached on national or world poverty; those with multilateral and non-interventionist foreign policy views were those who most commonly preached on the United Nations and world peace.

The clergy themselves recognized that their political attitudes affected their ministerial activities: 64 per cent agreed that they did. And the lower the score on doctrinalism, the larger the proportion agreeing (93 per cent of those who scored zero agreed, while only 38 per cent of those who scored 4 did so).

From the findings in this chapter it becomes obvious that to enlist the power of the pulpit in the struggle for social justice, reform, and a humane society poses a much more complicated problem than has been recognized. Where we have worried about sermons falling on deaf ears, we now see that a substantial problem exists in the silence of the majority of the pulpits. And where we have thought the problem was to arouse the clergy to action and to help them find more effective ways of reaching the laity, we now see that a prior problem is that much of the silence of the clergy is rooted in theology. In short, the data indicate that we have been misled in perceiving the failures of the churches to guide society on moral and ethical issues of social import as mainly a lay phenomenon. The clergy demand at least equal concern.

Yet, if the majority are silent, we must acknowledge that there is also an outspoken minority among clergy. Perhaps it is both unrealistic and unnecessary to expect more than this—unrealistic because activism is almost always a minority phenomenon, whatever the context, whatever the group examined; unnecessary because the outspoken clergy may be the vanguard of far-reaching changes in our religious institutions and thus important far beyond their numbers. To conclude this chapter, we must consider this latter possibility.

The "New Breed"

Much has been written in the past few years about the rapid and widespread changes assumed to be occurring in religious institutions. It is generally agreed that we are in the midst of a "New Reformation." Furthermore, it is widely believed that a "New Breed"[18] of younger clergy have entered the churches and are the dynamic behind changes which, it is hoped, will result in a regenerated church that is relevant, responsive, engaged, and humane.

There can be no doubt that the New Breed exists. There is evidence that they have made considerable headway in campus and experimental ministries and even in denominational headquarters and administrative positions.[19] But, as we shall see below, our data suggest that the New Breed have made very little headway in the real organizational backbone of the church—the parish ministry. Although there are substantial numbers of what might be regarded as New Breed clergymen in some denominations, in the clergy as a whole their numbers have remained relatively small. Furthermore, there is reason to suspect that they are not growing.

The size of the New Breed depends somewhat on how one defines its membership, but, however defined, it seems to be very small. The two main defining criteria used in writings by and about the New Breed are a modernist theology and a commitment to social justice—a Christian witness in the world. Using only a theological definition, on the basis of the Doctrinal Index one could only argue that at most a third (31 per cent) of the clergy could be called New Breed (scores zero to 2), but a more realistic estimate might be in the neighborhood of one in ten. Turning to the criterion of exhibiting through action a strong commitment to social justice, the estimates remain about the same: 25 per cent of the clergy in this sample reported speaking out from their pulpits on controversial social and political issues as often as five times in the previous year. But, of course, some of this activity comes from theologically conservative clergymen. Thus, combining these very permissive criteria allows an estimate that no more than 12 per cent of the clergy in this sample can conceivably be called New Breed. There seem compelling grounds to think that the New Breed is especially common in California and that a nationwide estimate would probably be substantially smaller.[20]

Thus, at the moment the New Breed is a tiny minority. Of course, our data apply to only one point in time and could easily miss the fact of rapid growth in progress which had not yet reached sizable proportions in an absolute sense. A single, static picture of a rapid process is necessarily misleading. Thus we run the danger of pondering immutable statistics while the rapid growth in the real world goes by unnoticed.

Yet, if this is the case there ought to be some detectable signs. Instead, in our judgment, the signs point to a lack of growth, for it seems certain that the New Breed suffers from a high rate of defection. It is hardly news that a major crisis facing the churches is the fact that so many are leaving the clergy. Ministers, priests, nuns, and seminarians are quitting in large and growing numbers each year. It has not been possible to obtain reliable statistics on the size of defections, but many church officials have estimated that withdrawals from the clergy have been about 7 per cent a year recently. In the seminaries, both in terms of declining enrollments, dropouts, and graduates who do not enter the clergy, the decline is probably considerably greater.[21] The question is: Who is leaving? There is widespread evidence that it is mainly the New Breed. For one thing, many of the most prominent original New Breed leaders have themselves left. Data show that New Breed types have long tried to avoid the parish and have flowed into administrative positions, especially campus chaplaincies, and that it is also from these ranks that many defections come.[22] Our data do not directly bear on defection. All were still in the church at the time of the study. Yet, Table 35 provides strong indication that defection is endemic among the New Breed.

All clergymen were asked to reconsider their calling: "Looking back on things—if you had it do over—how certain are you that you would enter the ministry?" It seems a telling comment on the state of religious institutions that only just over half (56 per cent) had no regrets and would definitely do it again. More important, only 14 per cent of those who scored zero and 22 per cent of those who scored 1 believed they would definitely go into the clergy again, while 75 per cent of those who scored 4 on doctrinalism definitely would. The majority of the theological New Breed had second thoughts about their vocation. Indeed, 26 per cent of those who scored zero said they definitely or probably would not do it again—only 6 per cent of the whole Protestant clergy were this much disillusioned with being ministers.

Table 35.   DOCTRINALISM AND DISILLUSIONMENT

	Doctrinal Index					
	Low				High	
	0	1	2	3	4	Total
Number	(28)	(134)	(296)	(467)	(568)	(1,493)
"Looking back on things— if you had it to do over— how certain are you that you would enter the ministry?"						
Definitely would do it again	14%	22%	45%	54%	75%	56%
Probably would do it again	39	40	32	31	18	27
Not sure	21	19	15	13	4	11
Probably would not do it again	22	18	6	2	3	5
Definitely would not enter the ministry	4	1	2	0	0	1
	100%	100%	100%	100%	100%	100%

If defection is high and probably on the increase while recruitment is declining, and if both of these processes mainly affect the New Breed, the New Breed would seem to have been a short-lived phenomenon among the clergy and to have reflected rebellion, not revolution. The

"Old Breed" greatly predominate. It seems likely to us that they will increase their dominance if only through default—while the vanguard is being decimated, the rear guard proceeds unscathed.

Evidence that it is the New Breed who are most prone to leave the ministry coincides with evidence that among the laity it is those most inclined to theological modernism and ethical commitment who are drifting into inactivity or even out of the churches altogether.[23] Since such laymen represent the potential constituency of the New Breed, the fact of their defection and inactivity should have raised serious questions about the plausibility of the New Reformation which has been so widely taken for granted. As we have shown elsewhere, the backbone of lay support for the churches remains very conservative.[24] Jeffrey Hadden has suggested that the commitment of the clergy to refashioning the churches is bound to produce a profound struggle between the clergy and the laity who oppose such change—some signs of which have already appeared in church conflicts, clergy firings, the withholding of funds, and the like.[25]

Our data partly support his conclusions. Clergymen most likely to speak out from the pulpit on human and social issues or otherwise engage in activism are overwhelmingly theologically *and* politically liberal. Thus, a conservative lay constituency is confronted with clergy activism which runs counter to their own political and social views. Consequently clergy activism has become more or less synonymous in the minds of the laity with liberal activism, and this has, indeed, created considerable conflict over the proper role of the clergy. But, as our data show, the majority of the clergy are not really in conflict with the laity. They are not activists, either in the streets or in the pulpit, and their social and political views are quite conservative. Thus, the pressure against clerical activism is borne almost wholly by the New Breed, whose influence, in our judgment, is not sufficient to produce more than superficial changes in religious institutions. They appear to find cosmetic solutions unacceptable as a substitute for real reformation. Consequently, they will probably continue to leave out of frustration.

Of course, many of the leaders of the New Breed expect that this very frustration will be the source of radically new forms of ministry and will produce a transformation in the basic organization of the churches. They do not envision the possibility of reforming a church still based on a parish structure. Rather they dismiss such a structure as anachronistic and believe that the faster young clergymen abandon it for a ministry not rooted in an institutional base, the faster a regenerated church will emerge. In our judgment, this is naïve. It assumes a church without a structure for funding itself, for coordinating its activities, or through which to involve its constituents. A church not based on parishes has no way to organize its connections with the laity. Even a charismatic evangelist such as Billy Graham cannot gather his great rallies except through months of organizational effort based on the congregations in the local community. We cannot envision a church except of the most flimsy and tenuous kind not built on organized local units; and, of course, this is also true for social movements, political parties, or any other large-scale effort to mobilize people. Indeed, we believe that the New Breed have dismissed the parish church mainly because of their failure to make significant inroads in this sector of the churches. Rather than a portent of a new institutionless church, their turn to secular society and away from organized religion seems a sign of the immovability of religious institutions.

So where does that leave those who wish to enlist the churches in efforts to eradicate social evils? The only workable answer we can offer is predicated on dealing with the churches as they really are, not with some hoped-for vision of the future. Efforts must be concentrated on the silent majority. We have elsewhere commented that it is difficult to maintain a realistic view of the religious situation if one often attends conferences and symposiums on problems of peace, race, and the like in which religious spokesmen participate.[26] The majority of such clerical participants are filled with moral fervor and compassion and seek an active Christian witness on such matters. One is easily misled into thinking of them as representative of moral ferment in the churches and as certain evidence that the churches are a potentially powerful force in such matters. This is always the danger in preaching to the converted; as many important evangelists have recognized, it prevents you from reaching the heathen. Thus, in our judgment it is vital now to turn away from the comforts of dialogues with the New Breed and seek conversations with the main body of the clergy.

So long as efforts to arouse the average parish clergymen on such human issues as peace, poverty, prejudice, and justice are no more successful than they have been so far, Sunday will remain the same: the American silent majority sitting righteously in the pews listening to silent sermons.

Notes

1. Christian Beliefs and Anti-Semitism—Revisited

1. Charles Y. Glock and Rodney Stark (New York: Harper & Row, 1966).
2. For example, it is obviously unthinkable to test the assertions in the present study by randomly assigning babies to be raised as Christians or atheists and then contrasting their attitudes toward Jews and adults.
3. *Constructing Social Theories* (New York: Harcourt, Brace, and World, 1968).
4. Rodney Stark, "Psychopathology and Religious Commitment," *Review of Religious Research*, in press.
5. A full report on sampling methods and analysis of bias in returns is included in Harold E. Quinley, *The Prophetic Clergy: Social Activism Among Protestant Ministers*, unpublished Ph.D. dissertation, Dept. of Political Science, Stanford University, 1970.

2. Theological Convictions

1. The findings for laymen are not strictly comparable with those for clergy, since the former are based on a sample of laity in churches in four Northern California counties, whereas the latter constitute a sample of clergy in the entire state. It will be instructive, nevertheless, as we proceed to see whether the general thrust of the findings is concordant or discordant.
2. John A. T. Robinson, *Honest to God* (Philadelphia: Westminster, 1963); Paul Tillich, *Systematic Theology* (Chicago: University of Chicago Press, 1956).
3. As a matter of regular practice, we shall not report detailed findings by denomination for the laity since the interested reader can find them in *Christian Beliefs and Anti-Semitism*. They are presented here, however,

to illustrate their high concordance with the results for clergy. The same high concordance was found almost uniformly wherever comparisons were possible.

4. See Charles Y. Glock and Rodney Stark, *Religion and Society in Tension* (Chicago: Rand McNally, 1965), Chapter 5.

5. For a summary, see *ibid.*

6. "A Protestant Paradox—Divided They Merge," *Trans-Action* (July/August 1967).

7. For more extended discussion of the material in this section, see Rodney Stark and Bruce D. Foster, "In Defense of Orthodoxy: Notes on the Validity of an Index," *Social Forces,* Vol. XLVIII, No. 2 (March 1970).

8. In the laymen study, two versions of the Orthodoxy Index were used. In the national sample, belief in life after death was substituted for the item on faith in Biblical miracles. In the present study, belief in life after death was the version of the index used.

9. Charles Y. Glock and Rodney Stark (New York: Harper & Row, 1966).

10. Rodney Stark and Charles Y. Glock (Berkeley and Los Angeles: University of California Press, 1968).

11. Of course, measurement is nearly always improved to some extent by increasing the number of items (if they are equally valid). The reason for using as few as can measure adequately is that survey studies must be kept reasonably short and consequently items devoted to one topic preclude the study of other topics.

12. This is important because while either measure can be used among clergymen, only the Orthodoxy Index is usable among the laity. That the index is interchangeable with clergymen's self-conceptions greatly increases confidence in using the Orthodoxy Index among laymen.

13. Atheists, for example, are not identifiable by their names or their ethnicity.

14. We use this term as it was used by the Southern Baptist president. We recognize that it is not entirely appropriate and mainly reflects the fact that *he thinks of Jews as a race.* We hardly argued that Christians exclude Jews on racial grounds; rather that they hold invidious views of Jews who fail to convert to Christianity.

3. Religious Conceptions of the Jews

1. As this was written, the Roman Catholic Church was considering adopting a further statement on Catholic-Jewish relations which would greatly enlarge this basis.

2. Charles Y. Glock, Benjamin B. Ringer, and Earl R. Babbie, *To Comfort and to Challenge* (Berkeley and Los Angeles: University of California Press, 1967).

3. For a summary of these studies, see Charles Y. Glock and Rodney Stark, *Christian Beliefs and Anti-Semitism* (New York: Harper & Row, 1966), Chapter 1.

4. The Religious Hostility Index was scored as follows: On each statement "Strongly agree" was scored 4, "Agree" 3, "No opinion" 2, "Disagree" 1,

and "Strongly disagree" 0; thus the full range of one index was from zero (for strongly disagreeing with both statements) to 8 (for strongly agreeing with the two items). To facilitate analysis, however, the index was subsequently collapsed. The zero category remained the same, scores of 1 and 2 were combined as 1, scores 3 and 4 combined as 2, and scores 5, 6, 7, and 8 combined as 3.

5. The Doctrinal Index was constructed as follows: The Orthodoxy Index was recoded from zero through 4 to zero through 2 thus: Zero remained unchanged, scores 1, 2, and 3 were collapsed together as 1, and score 4 was recoded to 2. On the particularism item respondents received a score of 2 for saying "Belief in Jesus Christ as Saviour" was "absolutely necessary for salvation," 1 for "would probably help in gaining salvation," and 0 for "probably had no influence on salvation." Only respondents who scored 2 (maximum) on both orthodoxy and particularism were scored in answer to the question "Which group do you think was most responsible for crucifying Christ?" If those who already scored 4 answered "The Jews" they were rescored 5; if they answered "The Romans," "The Greeks," "The Christians," "None of these," or "don't know" they remained scored 4.

4. Secular Anti-Semitism

1. See Rodney Stark and Charles Y. Glock, *American Piety: The Nature of Religious Commitment* (Berkeley and Los Angeles: University of California Press, 1968), and Milton Rokeach, "Religious Values and Social Compassion," *Review of Religious Research* (Fall 1969).

2. The perils of sociology in contrast to anthropology were made quite obvious by one of the clergymen taking part in this study. When one studies primitive tribes one rarely has to confront a member of a tribe who is aware of an earlier study of yours. But consider the following comments written across the page in the questionnaire devoted to attitudes toward Jews by a respondent who refused to answer any of these questions: "This page ought to be omitted. The results will be unfair to Christian clergy whatever the answers. This is the type of thing Glock did at U.C. only his questions seemed very slanted [the questions were, of course, worded identically in both studies]. . . . Every person has prejudices if he is honest. After gathering this data, you will be able to say that clergymen have this as their attitudes toward Jews. But you made the statements. We just step on the trigger of the trap."

   In reply, either this clergyman could have taken the option provided to answer "no" to all five questions, or, as he said, if he is honest, he would have indicated his prejudices.

3. See Gertrude J. Selznick and Stephen Steinberg, *The Tenacity of Prejudice: Anti-Semitism in Contemporary America* (New York: Harper & Row, 1969).

4. Glock wrote the item. Stark was sure it wouldn't work.

5. For an extended discussion of this phenomenon, see Rodney Stark and Stephen Steinberg, "Jews and Christians in Suburbia," *Harper's* (Au-

gust 1967), and (by the same authors) "It *Did* Happen Here: An Investigation of Political Anti-Semitism," Anti-Defamation League of B'nai B'rith Monograph, No. FR8, 1967.

6. Categories 1 and 2—degrees of hostility toward Jews—have been collapsed since No. 1 drew only 10 respondents.

7. DXY $= .488$, $r = .592$, gamma $= .691$, and Q $= .806$. References are as follows: Measures of association (gamma and DXY), see Somers, "A New Asymmetric Measure," *American Sociological Review*, XXVII, 799; Goodman and Kruskul, "Measures of Association," *Journal of the American Statistical Association*, XLIX, 732, and LIV, 123. Correlation statistics (Pearsonian *r* and Kendall's Q), see Blalock, *Social Statistics* (1960).

8. The statistical logic involved is not commonly understood. Consequently, when similar manipulations were reported in *Christian Beliefs and Anti-Semitism* they led some critics to believe that there was no true relationship between doctrinalism and secular anti-Semitism. Nothing could be further from the truth. On the contrary, it had been shown *why* doctrinalism was related to secular anti-Semitism.

To avoid further misunderstanding, it seems prudent to try once more to explain the underlying logic. What we are arguing is that X (doctrinalism) causes T (religious hostility toward Jews) which causes Y (secular anti-Semitism), or, put another way, the means through which X causes Y is T. Consider a more obvious example. A bullet in the heart is diagnosed as the cause of a man's death. But there are various physiological linkages between the cause and the effect. Death resulted from the bullet *because* the bullet did severe tissue damage to the heart, the heart could no longer circulate the blood, the blood thus could not carry oxygen to the brain and other organs, the organs failed for lack of oxygen, and the whole organism died because it was deprived of the normal function of these vital organs. Bullets striking bodies do not necessarily cause death. They do so only when they produce sufficient damage to vital organs so that the body can no longer sustain the life processes.

To pursue this logic, if we were to study a number of people who have been shot, we would find that death results *only* in cases where sufficient damage to vital tissues was done, while shots in nonvital portions of the anatomy do not result in death. Furthermore, when similar damage occurs in the same vital organs of persons who have not been shot, death will also result. Thus, if damage to organs is held constant, those not suffering such damage should continue to live whether or not they have been shot, and those suffering such damage should die regardless of whether or not they have been shot. Holding the intervening mechanism constant statistically wipes out the original correlation between being shot and dying. When this is found empirically to be the case, there is strong evidence that what has been postulated to be the linking mechanism is, in fact, such a mechanism.

9. Otis Dudley Duncan, "Path Analysis: Sociological Examples," *American Journal of Sociology*, Vol. LXXII, No. 1 (July 1966).

10. Correlation Matrix of the Relationships Between the Five Variables (Lay Sample)

	Orthodoxy	Particularism	Historic Jew	Religious Hostility	Anti-Semitism
Orthodoxy	X	.364	.162	.383	.075
Particularism		X	.058	.357	.146
Historic Jew			X	.170	.031
Religious Hostility				X	.218
Anti-Semitism					X

Table of Normalized[a] Regression Coefficients (Direct Path Coefficients) (Lay Sample)

	Orthodoxy	Particularism	Historic Jew	Religious Hostility	Anti-Semitism
Orthodoxy	X	.364	.163	.273	−.032
Particularism		X	−.001	.251	.087
Historic Jew			X	.043	−.001
Religious Hostility				X	.200
Anti-Semitism					X

[a] All indices were run in their original uncollapsed form and were represented as real ordinal variables except for the responsibility for the Crucifixion of Christ item, which was dichotomized as the Jews/Others and was represented in the system as a nominal variable. Normalization is necessary in order to counteract discrepancies between indices due to their sheer size. (Variables are normalized [or standardized] in terms of their means and standard deviations from a normal probability table. A normalized variable has a mean of zero and a standard deviation of 1. The mean plus or minus 1 standard deviation includes 68 per cent of observations.) Crudely, indices with greater ranges are squashed and indices with smaller ranges are stretched in order to make them directly comparable.

11. Correlation Matrix of the Relationships Between Orthodoxy, Particularism, Historical Conceptions of the Jews as Crucifiers, Religious Hostility, and Anti-Semitism (Clergy Sample)

	Orthodoxy	Particularism	Historic Jew	Religious Hostility	Anti-Semitism
Orthodoxy	X	.516	.104	.467	.225
Particularism		X	.108	.329	.151
Historic Jew			X	.165	.160
Religious Hostility				X	.348
Anti-Semitism					X

Table of Normalized Regression Coefficients (Direct Path Coefficients) (Clergy Sample)

	Orthodoxy	Particularism	Historic Jew	Religious Hostility	Anti-Semitism
Orthodoxy	X	.516	.066	.398	.074
Particularism		X	.074	.111	.004
Historic Jew			X	.076	.070
Religious Hostility				X	.295
Anti-Semitism					X

5. Ministers as Moral Guides: The Silent Majority

1. Jeffrey K. Hadden, *The Gathering Storm in the Churches* (Garden City, N.Y.: Doubleday, 1969).
2. "Religious Values and Social Compassion," *Review of Religious Research* (Fall 1969).
3. Rodney Stark and Charles Y. Glock, *American Piety: The Nature of Religious Commitment* (Berkeley and Los Angeles: University of California Press, 1968); and Charles Y. Glock, Benjamin B. Ringer, and Earl R. Babbie, *To Comfort and to Challenge* (Berkeley and Los Angeles: University of California Press, 1967).
4. The base for computations was forty-eight sermons given per year, allowing for ministers to spend a month on vacation. This, of course, is a conservative estimate since in many denominations, especially those which are more conservative, ministers give several sermons a week.

5. Data supporting this point will appear in Harold E. Quinley, *The Prophetic Clergy: Social Activism Among Protestant Ministers*, unpublished Ph.D. dissertation, Dept. of Political Science, Stanford University, 1970.

6. We have eliminated data on ministers who claimed to have "touched upon" one or more of these topics during a sermon. Careful analysis showed that those who only touched upon such a topic very closely resembled those who remained utterly silent when it came to taking any other forms of action of these issues; they were unlikely to discuss them informally, to write letters to political leaders, to organize or attend study groups on these matters, and so on. Those who did do more than touch upon such matters were relatively likely to take such additional actions as well. As has already been shown, devoting a sermon mainly to these topics can mean little enough; it may include not even taking a stand. In our judgment the data show that touching upon such a topic means virtually nothing in terms of speaking out from the pulpit on such issues.

7. A group of the state's most respected physicians had been brought up on charges before the medical board on charges of illegal abortion on women who had contracted German measles early in their pregnancies. In the midst of this dispute serious efforts went forth in the legislature to liberalize the existing abortion law—an effort that was successful.

8. See Hadden, *op. cit.*

9. Quinley, *op. cit.*

10. The item concerning historic Jewish guilt for the Crucifixion was dropped from the index as obviously irrelevant to the matters under study.

11. Langdon Gilkey, "Social and Intellectual Sources of Contemporary Protestant Theology in America," *Daedalus* (Winter 1967).

12. Glock, Ringer, and Babbie, *op. cit.*

13. Rodney Stark and Charles Y. Glock, "Prejudice and the Churches," in Charles Y. Glock and Ellen Siegelman (eds.), *Prejudice USA* (New York: Praeger, 1969).

14. Item 1 was scored: "Strongly agree" 3; "Agree" 2; "Disagree" 1; "Strongly disagree" 0; "No opinion" respondents dropped from index; items 2 and 3 were also scored 3 through 0, but in reverse order. Thus, the full index ranged from zero through 9. Four analysis scores were collapsed as follows: 0 = None; 1, 2, and 3 = Low; 4 and 5 = Medium; and 6, 7, 8, and 9 = High.

15. Full particulars on Somers DXY appear in Chapter 4, fn. 8. We have chosen to present Somers DXY results because they proved to be the most conservative estimate of the measures computed. In all cases r, G, and Q showed higher initial correlations and greater reductions when controls were introduced. Thus we have chosen to maximize the difficulty of establishing our case, which is as it should be.

16. Quinley, *op. cit.*

17. *Ibid.*

18. Harvey Cox, "The 'New Breed' in American Churches: Sources of Social Activism in American Religion," *Daedalus* (Winter 1967).

19. Phillip E. Hammond, *The Campus Clergyman* (Garden City, N. Y.: Doubleday, 1966); Hadden, *op. cit.*; and Phillip E. Hammond and Robert E.

Mitchell, "Segmentation of Radicalism: The Case of the Protestant Campus Minister," *American Journal of Sociology*, LXXI (1965), 133–143.

20. A comparison between California clergymen and their colleagues nationwide can be made by reference to Hadden, *op. cit.* Such a comparison shows that California clergy in all denominations are more liberal and activist than are clergy elsewhere.

21. For the first time in a decade, seminary applications and enrollments rose for the academic year 1969–1970. Leading seminary deans candidly admitted, however, that this seemed wholly caused by young men wanting to avoid the draft.

22. Hammond and Mitchell, *op. cit.*, and Hadden, *op. cit.*

23. Stark and Glock, *American Piety.*

24. *Ibid.*

25. Hadden, *op. cit.*

26. Stark and Glock, "Prejudice and the Churches."

INDEX

Index

71 72 73 74 10 9 8 7 6 5 4 3 2 1